RACIAL MYTH IN ENGLISH HISTORY

Trojans, Teutons, and Anglo-Saxons

HARVEST HOUSE
Montreal
UNIVERSITY PRESS OF NEW ENGLAND
Hanover and London

1982

RACIAL MYTH IN ENGLISH HISTORY

Trojans, Teutons, and Anglo-Saxons

HUGH A. MacDOUGALL

Published simultaneously by
HARVEST HOUSE LTD.
4795 St. Catherine Street, W.
Montreal, Canada, H3Z 1S8

and the

UNIVERSITY PRESS OF NEW ENGLAND
Hanover, New Hampshire 03755

Deposited in the Bibliothèque Nationale of Quebec, 2nd quarter 1982

Typography and Cover: Book Design and Production Associates, Bynum, N.C.

Printed in the U.S.A.

CANADIAN CATALOGUING IN PUBLICATION DATA

MacDougall, Hugh A., 1922-
Racial myth in English history

Bibliography: p.
Includes index.
ISBN 0-88772-211-3 (bound)
ISBN 0-88772-212-1 (pbk.)

1. Ethnology–Great Britain. I. Title.

DA120.M.32 942.01 C82-090023-0

LIBRARY OF CONGRESS CATALOGING IN PUBLICATION DATA

MacDougall, Hugh A.
Racial myth in English history.

Includes index.
1. British–Origin. 2. Anglo-Saxon race.
3. Geoffrey, of Monmouth, Bishop of St. Asaph, 1100?-1154. 4. Great Britain–History–To 1066–Historiography. 5. Mythology, British. I. Title.
DA135.M15 942.01 81.69941
ISBN 0-87451-228-X AA AACR2
ISBN 087451-229-8

To Beverly, Alanna, and Colin

CONTENTS

ACKNOWLEDGMENTS

I have received fruitful suggestions and advice from many persons in the preparation of this study. Special mention must be made of the invaluable assistance of two of my colleagues at Carleton University, Mark Phillips and James Noonan. They have saved me from many errors; for any that may remain I alone am responsible. I also express thanks to the staff of the Institute of Historical Research and the librarians of the University of London for a constant cooperation in the initial preparation of this work. Finally, I take this opportunity to express a life-long debt to the late Sir Herbert Butterfield, my supervisor and mentor during my graduate years at Cambridge, who first introduced me to the fascinating complexities of Whig history.

This book has been published with the help of a grant from the Canadian Federation for the Humanities, using funds provided by the Social Sciences and Humanities Research Council of Canada.

INTRODUCTION

Myths of origin enable people to locate themselves in time and space. They offer an explanation of the unknown and hallowed traditions by linking them to heroic events and personages of the distant past. In addition, they form the ground for belief systems or ideologies which, providing a moral validation for attitudes and activities, bind men together into a society.

In English history two national myths predominate. The first, best represented in a twelfth-century work by Geoffrey of Monmouth, a Welsh bishop, located the origins of the early inhabitants of Britain in Troy. Of special significance to the Welsh, who claimed to be the chief protectors of the ancient British inheritance, Geoffrey's *History of the Kings of Britain*, with its magnificent embellishment of the Arthurian legend, was guaranteed survival as the enduring romance of Celtic Britain.

Geoffrey of Monmouth lived in close association with both the English and the Normans and his account was written with them in mind. It was quickly perceived that his famous *History* could be bent to serve multiple political purposes (its dynastic implications are still preserved in the title, Prince of Wales). The Geoffrian account of origins was widely accepted throughout the late Middle Ages, but the advent of the Renaissance and the Reformation brought its credibility under attack. It had its defenders in the seventeenth century, but with the confirmation of the Glorious Revolution its political vitality was spent. The first part of my account will concentrate on the content and fate of this remarkable book.

The second great national myth, asserting the Teutonic or Anglo-Saxon origins of Englishmen, claimed a higher degree of historicity than Geoffrey's account. It arose in the sixteenth century in response to complex religious and political needs, matured over the succeeding three centuries in step with England's rise to imperial status, and suffered decline in our own century.

It is the genesis and growth of the latter myth, variously referred to as Anglo-Saxonism, Teutonism, Gothicism, that will receive the major attention of this study. In its most highly developed form it has four postulates:

1. Germanic peoples, on account of their unmixed origins and universal civilizing mission, are inherently superior to all others, both in individual character and in their institutions.
2. The English are, in the main, of Germanic origin, and their history begins with the landing of Hengist and Horsa at Ebbsfield, Kent, in 449.
3. The qualities which render English political and religious institutions the freest in the world are an inheritance from Germanic forefathers.
4. The English, better than any other Germanic people, represent the traditional genius of their ancestors and thereby carry a special burden of leadership in the world community.

The above themes or their variants are at the heart of Anglo-Saxonism. For its committed advocate the concept of race is central. (Though the term race defies precise definition, in its primary sense it has reference to the common biological origins of a particular people). Until the twentieth century few questioned the appropriateness of using racial terminology in reference to the various peoples of Europe. While it is now recognized that if the test of common genetic origin is applied there is no German, English, Irish, Aryan, or Jewish race—tribal migrations and intermarriage preclude the possibility—earlier generations hardly shared this perception. Yet, the power of myths and their related ideologies lies not in their objective truth but in their being perceived as true. By mid nineteenth century most Englishmen uncritically accepted the basic tenets of Anglo-Saxonism. At the height of Victorian imperialism it seemed abundantly manifest that England's triumph grew out of its blessed inheritance. Little time was given to reflection on the human exploitation involved in achieving such a high level of imperial greatness.

Though by the early decades of the twentieth century few specialists in any field supported ethnic theories asserting the inherent superiority of any particular people, still the earlier racial dogmas remain to this day deeply embedded in popular culture and require only a slight prod to rise to the surface.

The present work seeks to review the development of the two most significant myths of origin in English history. The transition from one ideology to the other was neither an abrupt nor a smooth flowing one, but involved complex and often conflicting historical factors spanning several centuries. The developing sense of nationalism helps explain the greater coherence and ultimate triumph of the Germanic myth, for it arose and matured in response to the needs of a restless people unconsciously pursuing a road that led to national and imperial greatness. Throughout the book, extensive use is made of citations from contemporary writers. The historically conscious general reader should find rewarding even a brief contact with authors of earlier ages, including many with whose work he is probably unfamiliar. Finally, it is the author's hope that the work will make some contribution toward a clearer recognition of those elements in accepted mythologies which tend to divide men.

Chapter I

THE BRITONS AS TROJANS

The Legendary World of Geoffrey of Monmouth

In the history of myths of national origin few have been as influential and have had such a curious development as those popularized by Geoffrey of Monmouth in his *History of the Kings of Britain.* His writing, appearing about 1136, was destined to become "the most famous work of nationalistic historiography in the Middle Ages."[1] It had a marked influence in subduing the social animosities of the Bretons, Anglo-Saxons, and Normans and drawing them together into a single nation. Geoffrey's fanciful account was used by early Plantagenet monarchs to support their regal claims and for both Tudors and Stuarts it came to constitute a useful prop to their dynastic ones. Though confidence in its historical reliability had almost evaporated by the eighteenth century, as the chief source of the Arthurian legend its influence carried on into the nineteenth century and as a spur to Celtic imagination continues into our own day.

The author of the famous *History* was a Welsh cleric, probably of Breton descent, who a few years before his death became Bishop of St. Asaph. At the outset of his book Geoffrey acknowledged his debt to Walter, Archdeacon of Oxford, who had provided him with "a very ancient book written in the British language" which related the actions of the British kings "from Brutus, the first king of the Britons, down to Cadwallader" the last.[2] At Archdeacon Walter's request, so writes Geoffrey, a Latin translation of the ancient book is offered the reader.

Since no corroborating evidence for the existence of Walter's "*vetustissimus liber*" has ever come to light, one may credit Geoffrey's colorful *History* to a fertile imagination fed by contemporary oral traditions and accounts by earlier scribes like Gildas and Nennius.[3] Geoffrey's motivation in writing his book no doubt was a desire to provide an heroic epic on the origin and exploits of a people subdued successively by Romans, Saxons, Danes, and Normans. By portraying the British as a once great people with extensive dominions he could at once raise their status in the eyes of their new Norman overlords and suggest a precedent to the Norman kings in their imperialistic ambitions. Geoffrey's success can be measured by the gradual acceptance of his account as a great national myth supporting a developing people moving toward nationhood.

In locating the origin of British history in ancient Troy Geoffrey was following an accepted tradition. The dignifying of one's own history by associating its beginnings with an earlier civilization or even with the gods was a practice well known to classical writers. Rome provided a model ready at hand. Its patriotic writers, admiring Greek civilization though disliking the Greeks, chose as their mythical hero Aeneas, son of Venus, a chief defender of Troy. Vergil in his great Latin epic, the *Aeneid*, portrayed him after various heroic exploits as the founder of *Lavinium*, the parent city of Rome. The Gallo-Romans as well as the Franks in Gaul drew on the tradition of Trojan origins, as, in time, did the Normans. Geoffrey in his *History* simply exploited an existing myth which was guaranteed to sit well with the Norman masters of England.[4]

The *History* begins with an account of the birth and upbringing of Brutus, grandson of Aeneas of Troy, son of Venus. Held responsible for his mother's death in childbirth and the accidental killing of his father, the fifteen-year-old boy was banished from his country. After many wanderings and heroic exploits, Brutus arrived with his faithful followers in the land *Albion*, to which he gave his own name, Britain. The land had fine rivers and forests and was inhabited only by a few giants. The giants were conquered, the land occupied and a city called New Troy (*Trinoventum*) founded. After their leader, the new inhabitants were called Britons and their language British.

Twenty years following his arrival on the island Brutus died, leaving Britain divided among his three sons—the eldest holding England, the second son Scotland, and the youngest Wales. Upon the death of the younger sons the entire land reverted to the eldest, Locrinus. The *History* continues with the heroic exploits of a long line of kings including the famous account of King Leir and his three daughters—a romantic tale subsequently retold by at least fifty writers before Shakespeare immortalized it.

Among some of the more notable British kings descended from the original Trojans were Belinus and Brennius who shared a divided kingdom and together conquered Gaul. Brennius occupied Rome and exercised there an unheard of tyranny, such was his might. Another, King Lud, rebuilt the walls of New Troy and gave it his name, which through the corruption of language became known as London. During the reign of Lud's successor, King Cassivelaunus, Julius Caesar turned his gaze on Britain. Caesar recognized the common descent from the Trojans of both Romans and Britons but the latter he judged degenerate, knowing nothing of the art of war and separated from the rest of the world. He accordingly demanded tribute and submission to Rome, a demand stoutly resisted by the Britons.

The next king, Arviragus, was reconciled with the Romans and married the daughter of the Emperor Claudius. The reign of his grandson, Lucius, was notable for the conversion of his kingdom, making Britain the first of all nations publicly to profess Christianity. He was buried in Gloucester Cathedral in A.D. 156–the first precise date given by Geoffrey.

Constantine I was another luminary in the ranks of the British kings. With the support of Roman exiles he captured Rome, overthrew the tyrant Maxentius and was made overlord of the whole world. Upon Constantine's death the treacherous Vortigern became king. Instead of resisting the incursions of the infidel Saxons he accepted their offer of service. Infatuated by Renwein, the beautiful daughter of the Saxon leader Hengist, he came to love the Saxons above all other peoples. The influx of Saxons became so great that the Britons overthrew Vortigern in favor of his son Vortimer who forced the Saxon warriors back to Germany. But following the death of Vortimer, his father once more became king and invited the Saxons to return. Hengist landed with an army of 300,000 men and a great massacre of Britons ensued.

Confronted with a ravaged kingdom, Vortigern sought counsel from magicians. Geoffrey relates at length the king's association with the magician Merlin and the seer's predictions concerning the future history of Britain. The prophecies are filled with imagery of dragons in conflict—the white dragon (Saxons) is initially victorious, but ultimately vanquished by the red dragon (Britons) through the assistance of a people dressed in wood and in iron corselets (Normans in their ships and coats of mail).

As foretold by Merlin, a champion of British and Roman ancestry, Aurelius Ambrosius, appeared to overthrow Vortigern and reduce the Saxons. Upon his death the work of restoration was continued by his brother, Utherpendragon, until he was poisoned by the Saxons. The climax of Geoffrey's entire *History* is reached with the ascendancy of Utherpendragon's illegitimate son, Arthur. King Arthur is clearly Geoffrey's hero. The remarkable success and continuing influence of his *British History* is due in no small measure to his brilliant portrayal of a British king with qualities well beyond the ordinary human—the stuff of which great myths are born.

Crowned king at the age of fifteen, Arthur was a youth of unparalleled courage and generosity. In time he subdued the Saxons —in one battle killing 470 with his own hand—forced the Scots and Picts to make peace, conquered Ireland, Iceland, the Orkneys, Sweden, Norway, Denmark, Aquitaine, and Normandy. The fame of his valor spread over the whole world. The splendor of his court was unrivaled and he eventually ruled over a kingdom that led the entire world in civilization.

In the meantime Rome grew alarmed at Arthur's growing power and his refusal to pay tribute. The Roman Procurator, Lucius Tiberius, demanded that Arthur report to Rome under the threat of his bringing the sword to Britain. Arthur refused and after consultation with his allies prepared for war. Lucius called upon the eastern kings for support. A host of kings with their generals and nobles—up to the number of forty thousand one hundred and sixty—pledged him support. Arthur then led his great army to Gaul to confront the Romans, leaving the government of his kingdom to his nephew Modred. In a great battle Lucius Tiberius was killed and the Britons were victorious. Many Romans subsequently offered themselves as slaves. Arthur then made preparations to march on Rome. As he approached the Alps news came that Modred had treacherously seized the Crown and taken Queen Guinevere as his wife. Arthur returned to Britain and in a resulting civil war Modred was killed. Arthur in the final battle was mortally wounded and carried to the magical isle of Avalon to be healed. He surrendered his crown to his kinsman Constantine, son of the duke of Cornwall, and passed out of the story. Geoffrey notes that the year was 542.

The reign of Constantine and his successors was beset with dissension and vice and the Saxons, aided by Gormund, King of the Africans, again overran the country. There was a brief revival of the hope of the Britons under the rule of the last British king, Cadwallader, but pestilence and famine forced them to leave the island altogether and take refuge in Brittany. Britain was now destitute of its ancient inhabitants except for a remnant in Wales. The Angles and Saxons had finally triumphed.

Cadwallader made plans to revive his kingdom, but was commanded by an angel to desist. He was instructed to go to Rome where, after penance, he would be enrolled among the saints. The Britons, so spoke the heavenly voice, would not recover their land until the time foretold by Merlin and decreed by God was come. Cadwallader, the last of the British kings, died in Rome on 12 May 689.

Geoffrey shrewdly ended his *History* with a warning to others to be silent concerning the British kings since they were not privy to the ancient book from Walter, Archdeacon of Oxford.

As a work of creative imagination Geoffrey's *History* was a superb achievement. Its heroic account of great deeds and dramatic failures salted with romantic intrigue and supernatural intervention was well designed to capture the medieval reader. By the time of his death in 1154 his account had been related so often that to be unfamiliar with it was, in the words of a contemporary, "to incur a mark of rusticity."[5] Paraphrases and translations abounded, among the most noteworthy of the early versions being *Geste des Bretons* (1155) by the poet Maistre Wace, dedicated to Eleanor, the wife of Henry II, and the *Brut* (c. 1200) by the English priest Layamon. Even Welsh writers, who possessed an Arthurian tradition predating Geoffrey, came to borrow much from him. Gradually his *History* became the foundation of a great historical myth which supported racial and dynastic aspirations for over five hundred years.

Still, several of the earliest critics were sceptical of the *History*'s authenticity. Alfred of Beverly (fl. 1143), a chronicler who was initially drawn to history through reading Geoffrey and had borrowed heavily from him in his own writings, was puzzled by the lack of corroboration for the *History* in writers outside of Britain.[6] Giraldus Cambrensis, a contentious Welsh historian, treated Geoffrey's account with disdain.[7] He told the tale of a Welshman who was beset by unclean spirits. When the spirits oppressed him the gospel of St. John was placed on his tormented breast, and they departed; but when Geoffrey's *History* was substituted for the gospel, the evil spirits returned to torment him in greater numbers than ever. The most categorical rejection, however, was made by William of Newburgh. In a preface to his *Historium Rerum Anglicarum* he dismissed Geoffrey's *History* as made up of "the most ridiculous fictions." "Whatever Geoffrey has written," he acidly comments, "is a fiction invented either by himself or by others, and promulgated either through an unchecked propensity to falsehood, or a desire to please the Britons, of whom vast numbers are said to be so stupid as to assert that Arthur is yet to come, and cannot bear to hear of his death." Newburgh noted that ancient historians were silent on the alleged Arthurian exploits: "It is plain that whatever this man published of Arthur and Merlin are mendacious fictions, invented to gratify the curiosity of the undiscerning." There was no doubt in William of Newburgh's mind how Geoffrey and his *History* should be treated: "Let this fabler, with his fictions, be instantly rejected by all."[8]

In spite of initial criticism, the *History* went on to triumph and came to be generally accepted until the Renaissance. Apart from the inherent attraction of a well-told tale dealing with origins, Geoffrey's *History* held special political appeal. A history presenting the extraordinary achievements of past British kings was calculated to please Norman conquerors (in Geoffrey's account also descended from Trojan exiles) who could now see themselves as inheritors of a kingdom with a proud past and notable achievements. Lacking any historical figure of heroic stature comparable to Charlemagne, the Norman and Angevin kings were in an inferior position to their continental French rivals. In Arthur, Geoffrey provided such a figure. Arthur in time served an additional function: more than Brutus or Cadwallader, he came to be seen as a hero of a composite people, uniting Britons, Saxons and Normans.[9]

From its beginnings Geoffrey's *History* was closely associated with the monarchy. One of the original manuscripts carried a dedication to Stephen who succeeded to the throne in 1135. Most of the manuscripts also included a dedication to Robert, Earl of Gloucester, a natural son of Henry I, who was to contribute much to the success of Henry II. The latter king was closely associated with the "discovery" of Arthur's body at the famous Benedictine monastery at Glastonbury. This renowned religious center, probably through the efforts of zealous monks who wished to increase its prestige, came to be identified as the mysterious isle of Avalon. King Henry, the chroniclers report, initiated the investigation which resulted in the discovery of the tomb and a subsequent magnificent reinterment.[10] Henry's motive in "arranging" the discovery need not have gone beyond his desire to put an end to the legend that Arthur was still alive and would return, a belief kept current by rebellious Welsh who dreamed of recovering national leadership. In 1187 King Henry had his grandson christened Arthur, the intended identification being obvious.

It was Edward I more than any of his predecessors who turned the *History* to his own advantage. He liked to cast himself in the role of "Arthurus redivivus."[11] In 1278, along with Queen Eleanor, he visited Glastonbury and ordered the opening of Arthur's tomb. A contemporary account tells of the extraordinary occasion: "The lord Edward . . . with his consort, the Lady Eleanor, came to Glastonbury . . . to celebrate Easter. . . . The following Tuesday . . . at dusk, the lord king had the tomb of the famous King Arthur opened. Wherein, in two caskets painted with their pictures and arms, were found separately, the bones of the said king, which were of great size, and those of Queen Guinevere, which were of marvellous beauty. . . . On the following day . . . the lord king replaced the bones of the king, and the queen those of the queen, each in their own casket, having wrapped them in costly silk. When they had been sealed they ordered the tomb to be placed forthwith in front of the high altar, after the removal of the skulls for the veneration of the people."[12]

Thus Edward succeeded magnificently in linking his own royal house with the most renowned of the ancient British kings and at the same time helped promote Glastonbury as a religious center to rival the fame of French abbeys like Cluny. Another Arthurian-Glastonbury association brought even further prestige and was appropriately exploited. The incorporation of St. Joseph of Arimathea through the Grail legend as the founder of a church in Glastonbury in A.D. 63 sanctioned the claim of an English church established in Apostolic times, a claim useful in the promotion of a national church less subject to the control of Rome.[13]

The advantage to Edward of the British connection was further demonstrated in 1301 in a jurisdictional dispute which the Scots brought to the court of Rome. In a letter to Boniface VIII, countersigned by a hundred English barons, Edward presented evidence to support the rights of the English crown over Scotland. Most of the evidence was drawn from Geoffrey's *History*.[14]

The young Edward III was no less enthusiastic for his British heritage. He contemplated reestablishing the Round Table and around 1348 founded the illustrious Order of the Garter, reviving the tradition of Arthurian knighthood.[15] He heavily patronized Glastonbury Abbey. Accompanied by his queen, he paid it a state visit in 1331. It has been suggested that his attempts to conquer France were influenced by the accounts of Arthur's continental conquests related in the *History*.[16] The reign of his namesake, Edward IV, a hundred years later, showed the enduring quality of the British legend. Genealogical authorities of his time traced his descent back to Cadwallader, the last of the British kings, and he was hailed by his supporters as the British Messiah, the Red Dragon foretold by Merlin who would once again rule England, Scotland and Wales.[17]

In the ninth year of Edward IV's reign (1469), Thomas Malory completed his epic work on Arthur. Derived more from twelfth-century French prose romances and a fourteenth-century English poem than from Geoffrey's *History* itself, it was published by William Caxton with considerable editorial liberty. Under the title *Morte d'Arthur* it became the best-known Arthurian account in English.[18] Interestingly, Caxton in his preface felt compelled to level sharp criticism at those who "holde oppynon that there was no suche Arthur and that alle suche bookes as bein maad of hym ben but fayned and fables."[19] Caxton had no time for Renaissance scepticism which led men like John Whethamstede, Abbot of St. Albans, to consider "the whole discourse of Brutus" to be "rather poeticall than historicall."[20] It is worth noting that the first printed book in the English tongue was *The Recuyell of the Historyes of Troye*, a translation from the French of Raoul Le Fèvrè's work. In 1480 Caxton printed the popular medieval account based on Geoffrey's *History*, *Chronicle of the Brut*, under the title *The Chronicles of England*. By the end of the century this work alone had appeared in six editions. Caxton, as well, printed Ranulf Higden's *Polychronicon*, a "universal history" containing much material on British history derived from Geoffrey. The *Polychronicon* and the *Brut* came to be by far the most widely read history books in fifteenth-century England.

The accession of Henry Tudor in 1485 was interpreted by many as the long awaited return of a British king in fulfillment of the ancient promise. It was under the banner of the Red Dragon that he had overthrown Richard III. In a welcoming pageant planned, but never actually held, for the new king at Worcester in 1486 an actor was to speak the following lines:

> Cadwalader Blodde lynyally descending,
> Long hath bee towlde of such a Prince comyng,

> Wherfor Frends, if that I shal not lye,
> This same is the Fulfiller of the Profesye.[21]

The Welsh were particularly enthusiastic, for their bards had frequently written of the coming of a great Welsh leader who would restore their ancient position.[22] But the most impressive testimony of Henry VII's special lineage came from the pen of Bernardus Andreas, the official historian of the new king. Andreas was an Augustinian friar from Toulouse who had come to England at the beginning of Henry's reign. He became the king's poet-laureate and historiographer, a useful combination from the regal point of view. In his *History of Henry VII* Andreas underlined Henry's British origins, tracing his royal descent from Cadwallader and portraying him as the fulfillment in his person of the ancient prophecy.[23] It appeared highly appropriate for the new king in 1486 to have named his first-born son after the great Arthur and thus heighten the promise of a new golden age. In 1548 the chronicler Edward Hall expressed what was still a popular sentiment when he wrote of Prince Arthur's christening at Winchester, a place noted for its Arthurian associations: "of whiche name Englishemen no more rejoysed than outwarde nacions and foreyne prynces trymbled and quaked, so muche was the name to all nacions terrible and formidable."[24] Writing in 1622, Francis Bacon noted the naming of Arthur, "according to the Name of that ancient worthy King of the Brittaines."[25]

In Tudor days belief in Trojan origins and reverence of King Arthur was by no means restricted to those who might justly claim British descent. Englishmen in general were heartened by tales of the legendary achievements of past British kings and, as T. D. Kendrick has written, "often extremely unwilling to acknowledge the barbaric Saxons as their ancestors, saw in the heroes and conquests of the Brut an obvious source of their country's pride and valiant heart."[26]

Henry VII's successor, Henry VIII, was at first far too concerned with establishing himself as a great monarch in his own right to be preoccupied with ancient tales of heroic achievements whose historicity his humanist friends were coming to question. (Humanists brought a more self-conscious approach to the study of political institutions, and the state gradually came to be seen as a formal structure distinct from any particular ruler.) Still the pageantry which Henry carried to the Field of the Cloth of Gold in 1520 spoke vividly of Arthur, the intrepid warrior of world renown.[27] Later in his reign when the great question of the divorce arose, a deliberate attempt was made to exploit Geoffrey's *History* to the King's advantage. In seeking to convince Charles V's ambassador of the justice of the king's plan for divorce, the duke of Norfolk, Henry's diplomatic spokesman, argued that his king held supreme imperial jurisdiction in his realm, a jurisdiction derived from ancient beginnings. The incredulous Chapuys was informed that Brennius, an Englishman, had conquered Rome, that Constantine had reigned in England and that, as well, his mother was English. In addition, an English monarch, Arthur (of whom Chapuys had never heard), had been Emperor of Britain, Gaul and Germany.[28] The ambassador's sardonic response that he regretted Arthur was not also called Emperor of Asia is understandable. The bold language in the preamble to the famous Act in Restraint of Appeals (1533), asserting that England was an empire "governed by one Supreme Head and King having dignity and royal estate of the imperial Crown," was dependent upon the tradition that Henry through the British kings was descended from the Emperor Constantine who was himself of half British origin and "had united British kinship with Roman emperorship."[29]

Ironically, the historian Polydore Vergil, whose work ultimately led to the destruction of the credibility of Geoffrey's entire history, undertook to write his history under the patronage of the first Tudor king and completed it under the second. Polydore Vergil was born at Urbino in the Romagna. He entered papal service and by the time he came to England in 1502 as a collector of Peter's Pence, he already had a reputation as a scholar. A friend of Erasmus, his world was that of the Renaissance, a movement barely beginning to make itself felt in England. He was not long there when, on the king's request, he began to work on a history of England. Henry VII, desirous of gaining European recognition of his dynasty, saw a new history designed for a continental readership and written in the best humanistic style as an asset which would enhance the king's reputation.[30]

From the beginning of his study, Vergil showed a complete disdain for Geoffrey's *History*. Though dutifully presenting a brief account of it for the sake of sensitive English readers ("They seem to be in heaven," he wrote, "where with good will I leave them,"), he approvingly cited William of Newburgh's characterization of it as "impudent lyeing."[31] He summarily dismissed the vaunted Trojan descent of the British through Brutus, the cornerstone of Geoffrey's *History:* "But yet neither Livie, neither Dionisius Halicarnaseus, who writt diligentlie of the Roman antiquities, nor divers other writers, did ever once make rehersall of this Brutus. . . ."[32] On the invasion of Rome by Brennius he noted that if the reference in the *History* was to the actual historical attack then in Geoffrey's version Brennius "lived 310 years before the battayle was taken in hande."[33] He devoted a single barbed paragraph to Arthur, presenting him as a mysterious man of romance and legend akin to Roland, a presentation certain to outrage Arthurian enthusiasts. He lightly rejected the claim that Arthur was buried in Glastonbury Abbey: "whereas in the dayse of Arthure this abbaye was not builded."[34]

Vergil's *Anglica Historia* was completed in 1513, but, despite the customary dedication to the king, twenty years were to elapse before it was published. (In the meantime in 1525 he had published an account of British history written in Anglo-Saxon times by Gildas in which King Arthur was not even mentioned.) Vergil's rejection of the British tradition could not help but displease the King. Henry's annoyance, it has been plausibly suggested, explains the long delay in its publication.[35] Its appearance in 1534 may be attributed to Henry's new situation. Having broken with Rome over the divorce issue Henry found it more important than ever to establish the imperial (and thus independent) nature of his crown in the eyes of continental rivals. The *Anglica Historia* in Renaissance fashion stressed the imperial nature of kingship and thus its appearance in 1534 served the king's purposes well. Significantly, Vergil's published version had a revised dedication and ending, both emphasizing, more than the original manuscript, Henry's imperial status.

Vergil's *Anglica Historia* was a work of impressive scholarship and could not be ignored. But his irreverent chiding of Englishmen on their view of the past evoked bitter hostility and mistrust among many scholars. His opponents tended to see him as an alien enemy set on furthering Rome's interests. The most impassioned attack came from the pen of the antiquarian John Leland.[36] He denounced "Polydorus the Italian" for his sceptical interpretation of Geoffrey's *History*, which he noted was "filled with Italian bitterness."[37] Especially worthy of reprobation was Vergil's presentation of Arthur who for Leland was "the chiefest ornament of Brittayne."[38] While admitting some absurdities had crept into the Arthurian account, he saw no reason why the presence of a few flaws weakened its overall credibility. So complete was Leland's commitment to the general line of Geoffrey's *History* that he offered a stout defense of Merlin—"a man even miraculously learned in knowledge of thinges naturall"—against the criticism "of any cowled or loytering grosseheaded Moncke" (a reference to William of Newburgh, whose authority Vergil had cited).[39] In concluding his defense Leland anticipated that "most mighty enemies will affaulte my doings," but he was confident that in the end, "the light of Brittish Antiquitie shall shine forth."[40] Another leading antiquarian and friend of Leland, Bishop John Bale, believed even more passionately in the authority of Geoffrey's *History*. Once a member of the Carmelite monastic order, he had joined the Protestant reformers and became violently anti-Roman. Bale charged Vergil with "polluting our English Chronicles most shamefully with his Romish lies and other Italian beggarys."[41] A more sober criticism came from Sir John Price, a Welsh lawyer, in his *Historiae Brytannicae Defensio*.[42] While recognizing Vergil's learning, he did not believe that the humanist had shaken Geoffrey's account. Other Welsh antiquarians like Humphrey

Lhuyd and David Powel were far less restrained in their condemnation of Vergil.[43]

By the last quarter of the century the popular image of Vergil was that of a scheming Italian papist who had insinuated himself into England by devious means and had proceeded to attack her most venerable traditions. "Polydore Vergil that most rascall dogge knave in the worlde," one angry commentator summed him up.[44] But the serious scholarship underlying Vergil's *Anglicana Historia* could not but impress conscientious readers. His scholarly method was in advance of any previous English historian. A scepticism born of the Renaissance prompted him to weigh authorities far more carefully than any contemporary English historical writer. The stimulus he provided for a more critical approach to sources was immense. His influence on the work of men like Edward Hall, Francis Bacon, and a whole range of later historians was considerable.[45]

Despite the vociferous defense of the British tradition by most English antiquarians there were a growing number of doubters. Five years before Vergil's history appeared, John Rastell, the antiquarian brother-in-law of Thomas More, commented that for some men of his day the story of Brutus was but "feyned fable."[46] For Rastell it was highly significant that Bede "spekyth nothyng of Arthur."[47] Though he went on to present in *The Pastyme of People* a brief version of Geoffrey's *History*, he would not vouch for its truth. Neither the antiquarians, John Twyne and George Lily, contemporaries of Leland, accepted the Trojan origin of the British, and the chronicler Thomas Lanquet was of the opinion that Geoffrey's *History* was full of errors.[48] There is no evidence that English humanists like Colet and More gave it credence.

During the Elizabethan age it was common to relate the English monarch to British antiquity, and pageantry and drama were filled with Arthurian imagery.[49] Spenser's *Faerie Queene*, linking Elizabeth to Arthur and heralding the advent of a new Golden Age, was an outstanding example of the continuing attraction the ancient British legend held for literate Englishmen.

It was the great Elizabethan and Jacobean antiquarian, William

Camden, who did more than any other native English writer to weaken the authority of Geoffrey's *History*. His *Britannia*, the first comprehensive topographical survey of Britain, appeared in 1586. It immediately established his reputation as an outstanding scholar and came to be recognized "as the crowning achievement of Tudor and early Stuart antiquarianism."[50] Within his lifetime six London editions of his history were published. In beginning his discussion of the origin of the British people, Camden dealt delicately with Geoffrey's *History*. He assured his readers that he did not seek "to discredit that history," but on the contrary sought to maintain it: "I have often strained my invention to the utmost to support it. Absolutely to reject it, would be to wage war against time, and to fight against a received opinion." But the cautious Camden went on at length to give reasons why so many "very learned and judicious men" rejected it.[51] His gentle attempt to appease the admirers of Geoffrey's *History* ill-concealed his scepticism. Since for Camden the origins of the name of Britain and its first inhabitants were so uncertain, and despite the efforts of scholars would probably remain so, he concluded he might justly treat Geoffrey's version as irrelevant.[52] Drawing on linguistic similarities, he was inclined to the opinion that the ancient Britons were of the same stock as the Gauls.[53] Yet he was not prepared to jettison Arthur, that "mighty bulwark of the British Government," and lamented that the age had not afforded "a panegyrist equal to his virtues."[54]

The latter years of Elizabeth's reign were marked by a growing anxiety over the question of succession. As it became apparent that Elizabeth would produce no heir, hopes for an orderly succession turned more and more on James VI of Scotland. His pedigree had much to offer Arthurian enthusiasts eager to herald a new Golden Age. It could be shown that he was of the line Brut, first through his grandmother, Margaret Tudor, but also through the male Stuart line reaching back to Llywelyn, the last native Prince of Wales. James, well acquainted with ancient British lore, accepted his role as fulfiller of Merlin's prophecy. He saw himself as a second Arthur who would restore the ancient unity of England and Scotland established by Brutus. James's accession was greeted with tumultuous joy in England and pageants joyously proclaimed his Arthurian ancestry.[55] Significantly, without the consent of parliament, he assumed the title of King of Great Britain—no mention being made of the separate kingdoms of Scotland and England.

The most eloquent champion of British antiquity and its continuity in the Stuart dynasty was the poet Michael Drayton. In his ardent work, *Poly-olbion* (1613), he defended "the long traduced Brute," as well as the seer Merlin and other notable figures out of the British tradition.[56] Geoffrey of Monmouth's stories, he protested, were not "idle tales . . . nor fabulous, like those devised by the Greeks."[57] Drayton took his stand as a fierce supporter of their literal truth: "I would restore Antiquity to Britain, and Britain to his Antiquity."[58] Though Drayton had the historian John Speed add historical notes to the *Poly-olbion*, the scepticism of the latter about much of Geoffrey's *History* did little to strengthen the poet's advocacy.

In spite of the new life given the *History* by James I and his supporters, doubts continued to be raised by antiquarians. Writing in 1607, Edward Ayscu discussed the origins of the first inhabitants of Britain and passed over Brutus and the Trojans as a fabrication "coyned in some Monkish mint about foure hundred years agone."[59] Drawing on Caesar and Tacitus he asserted "that the Britaines tooke beginning from their next neighbours the Gaules."[60] Ayscu's doubts about the *History* were more than matched by Peter Scriverius of Haarlem, who fervently pronounced it: "a great, heavy, long, thick, palpable and most impudent lie, and that so manifest as to need no refutation."[61]

In 1614 John Speed dedicated his *History of Great Britaine* to the new king as "Inlarger and Uniter of the British Empire. Restorer of the British name." Yet, after a careful assessment of the arguments for and against the theory of Trojan origins, he concluded with a call to Britons to, "disclaime their Brute, that bringeth no honour to so renowned a Nation, but rather cloudeth their glorie in the murder of his parents, and imbaseth their descents, as sprung from Venus, that lascivious adulteress."[62] If, Speed continues, "we will needs have our descents from the Trojans, may we not then more truly derive our blood from them through the Romans, who for the space of four hundred three score and six years were planted amongst us?" On Arthur he was more cautious, being prepared to "let Monmouth the Writer, Newberry the Resister and Leland the Retainer" speak for him.[63] But he believed Geoffrey's exaggerations deprived Arthur of "truly deserved honours."[64]

Sir Walter Raleigh, who brought out *The History of the World* in the same year as Speed's *History*, dealt more radically with early British history. Wishing to start where the facts were certain he began his outline with the Norman Conquest.[65]

In 1615 a stout defense of the Brut and Geoffrey's *History* was presented in John Stow's *The Annales*. In Stow's mind those who cast doubts on the *History* had much to answer for: "And the impugners of this ancient Historie must not with so light a breath, as they doe, seeme to blow away the authoritie of so many grave testimonies, the succession of so many Princes, the founders of so many monuments, and Lawes, and the ancient honors of the nation, that first with publike authoritie received Christianitie."[66] The chief villain for Stow was Polydore Vergil, who, "with one dash at a pen cashireth threescore Princes together, with all their histories and historians, yea and some ancient Lawes also."[67] Edmund Bolton in his *Hypercritica* (1618) was even more concerned about the consequences of sweeping away the *History:* "Nevertheless out of that very Story (let it be what it will) have Titles been framed in open Parliament, both in England, and Ireland, for the Rights of the Crown of England, even to entire Kingdoms. . . . If that Work be quite abolished there is a vast Blanck upon the Times of our Country, from the Creation of the World till the coming of Julius Caesar."[68] Bolton went on to calculate the positive support for the *History* against the opposition and concluded, "if the cause were to be try'd, or carried by Voices, the affirmative would have the fuller Cry."[69] His criteria for historical authenticity were broad indeed: "For my part I incline very strongly to have so much of every Historical Monument, or Historical Tradition maintain'd, as may well be holden without open absurdity."[70]

The concerns of men like Stow and Bolton that a challenge to traditional accounts of one's past represented a threat to the English system of government reflected the growing conflict between crown and parliament which was to reach its climax in the Civil War. In the main, Geoffrian enthusiasts sided with the King, while those who were cool to the ancient British accounts stressed parliamentary privileges. The latter turned more to Germanic sources for the fount of their traditional freedoms. Still, in spite of the emerging Saxon challenge, the vitality of the Geoffrian legend was far from spent and was to receive new life with the Restoration.

Charles II, a Stuart, who with as much right as his predecessors might claim to be a second Arthur, had learned to tread cautiously in asserting ancient prerogatives. Yet there were those who throughout his reign showed no reticence in trumpeting the cause of British antiquity. The antiquary Silas Taylor, in the course of establishing that, "Our English Laws are for the most part those that were used by the Antient Brytains," went out of his way to attack the "vulgar opinions" begun by Polydore Vergil that Geoffrey's *History* was fictitious. Geoffrey, Taylor triumphantly observed, "was the translator only of such a Language as Polydore did not understand."[71] That the Geoffrian account had popular appeal is suggested by the presentation of the play *The Destruction of Troy*. The author, the prolific dramatist John Bankes, anticipated that the specators, who were addressed as "London Trojans," would identify with events surrounding the fall of Troy. In the prologue it was noted that when Troy fell "its Remnant here did plant. And built this Place call'd it Troy-novant."[72]

It was the figure of Arthur that specially attracted Restoration writers. Perhaps the most spirited defense of his historicity was presented in Nathaniel Crouch's *The History of the Nine Worthies of the World* (1687). Arthur, it was recalled, was the seventh worthy in a line which included Hector of Troy, Alexander the Great, Julius Caesar, Joshua, David, Judas Maccabeus, Charlemagne and Godfrey of Bouillon. Of his many heroic deeds his most noteworthy was his conquering of the Saxons for Christianity. Crouch scornfully dismissed those who expressed disbelief in Arthur: "As it may be judged folly to affirm there never was any Alexander, Julius Caesar, Godfrey of Bullen, or Charlemagne, so may we be thought guilty of incredulity and ingratitude to deny or doubt the honourable Acts of our Victorious Arthur."[73] Crouch's work was well received and ran to three further editions by 1700.

The most significant writer to show an interest in Arthurian history as it related to the Stuart monarchy was John Dryden. (On Milton, see pp. 67-68.) He had the ambition to write a supreme epic poem. His theme would center on Arthur and as a poem of triumph would celebrate the descent of Charles II from Arthur, the greatest of the British kings. Other demands on his time prevented him from ever realizing his goal, but in conjunction with Henry Purcell he completed the dramatic opera, *King Arthur*, in 1684. However, it was not produced until 1691 and in the interval dramatic political changes had occurred that could be ignored at an author's peril. With the Stuarts deposed, Dryden was compelled to alter his text radically, dropping anything that might be interpreted as political allegory bearing on contemporary events. As he wrote to the Marquis of Halifax: "Not to offend the present time, nor a government which has hitherto protected me, I have been obliged so much to alter the first design, and to take away so many beauties from the writing, that it is now no more what it was formerly than the present ship of the Royal Sovereign, after so often taking down and altering, is the vessel it was at the first building."[74]

A bizarre adaptation of the Arthurian legend came at the end of the century in Sir R. D. Blackmore's epic poems *Prince Arthur* (1695) and *King Arthur* (1700). Hardly ever was political allegory made more obvious than in Blackmore's attempt to cast the events of the Glorious Revolution in an heroic mold. William of Orange, portrayed as the Christian Arthur, emerged as the bold champion of political freedom and true religion (Protestantism) against heathen Saxons (Catholics!). The Arthurian legend was suitably altered to accommodate all the major achievements of the Prince of Orange from his early career in the Netherlands, to his victory in England and his championing of the Protestant cause against Louis XIV.

Blackmore's poems represented a final effort by an English writer to make the ancient British legend serve a political purpose. Though interest in it continued well into the Augustan age—Alexander Pope toward the end of his life contemplated writing an epic on Brutus as the Trojan hero who established a great empire in Britain—the ancient myth had spent itself.[75] The seventeenth century had seen England moving from a monarchically based society with a Crown claiming an absolute authority derived from ancient prerogatives to a self-conscious nation dominated by landed and rising commercial interests with parliament seen as the principal center of political power. Old myths of origin stressing achievements of kings no longer served the interests of dominant groups and were pushed more and more into the realm of poetic fancy. The series of events which in the first half of the century culminated in the Civil War and in the second half in the Glorious Revolution amply demonstrated that a myth of origin more rooted in historical reality was required. There was one ready to hand that had taken form in the latter decades of the sixteenth century. The freedoms of Englishmen and past achievements in which they all might glory came more and more to be seen as proceeding along a path that led back not to Brutus, Troy, and the British kings, but rather to Saxon England and the forests of Germany. Anglo-Saxonism, born in the sixteenth century in response to a need to demonstrate an historical continuity for the national church, and nourished in the seventeenth in debates over royal supremacy, finally triumphed and became the dominant myth that fired the national imagination. The social utility of the legendary history of Geoffrey of Monmouth had expired.

Geoffrey's remarkable account of the Trojan origins of the British nation served Englishmen well for over five hundred years. Though finally rejected by an historically-conscious people, its influence carried into the nineteenth century in the writings of Wordsworth and Tennyson. The founding in our own century of the International Arthurian Society, with membership in thirty-three countries, attests to its continuing fascination for the modern reader.

Chapter II

THE RISE OF ANGLO-SAXONISM

Bede, the father of English history, writing in 731 observed: "This island at present, following the number of books in which the Divine law was written, contains five nations, the English, Britons, Scots, Picts and Latins, each in its own peculiar dialect, cultivating the sublime study of Divine truth."[1] It was manifestly clear to Bede that one of the five, the English, derived from the Germanic Angles, Saxons and Jutes, was elected by God to establish political hegemony. In the succeeding centuries, though Germanic social structures permeated the whole of the country and other races came to hold a very subordinate position, the anticipated political unity was never achieved: Danish invasions coupled with inter-tribal rivalry prevented it. Whatever national consensus there did exist was far more evident in the Roman-centered church than in the Saxon state.

The Norman Conquest in 1066 seemed to dispel forever the hope of an Anglo-Saxon England. Norman lords and the French tongue prevailed at court. The English language was so far discouraged "that it became practically the language of the illiterate, preserved among learned men only as a means of communication with the unlettered."[2] Within the church Roman forms were completely dominant. Even in the celebration of their past Englishmen gloried in the achievements of the ancient Britons. By far the most popular account of origins came not from the pen of a Saxon, but from a Breton writing in Latin who portrayed Germans as rude and barbarous. Throughout the High Middle Ages the Anglo-Saxon voice remained a muted one when heard at all. Then came the Reformation.

The sixteenth century was a watershed in English history. The Henrician reforms transformed a nation and compelled Englishmen to take a new look at their past. Rejecting the papal claim to imperial authority in the West, Henry VIII asserted a regal power as legitimate as that of Constantine. (Conveniently in 1534, there appeared an English translation of Lorenzo Valla's exposure of the Donation of Constantine purportedly granting the papacy supremacy over the entire Western world). The king's loyal subjects were no longer permitted to regard the papacy as the source from which the English church was derived and sustained. The regal challenge to the temporal and spiritual authority of the pope led reformers to reach back into the past to expose unwarranted papal claims and practices and eventually to deny doctrines held firmly by the reforming king himself.

Where was the autonomous English church before the Reformation? This became a central question reformers had to confront, if only to respond to insistent Roman Catholic apologists. The tradition of an early Christian establishment in the days of King Lucius, based on Geoffrey's *History of the Kings of Britain*, together with the associated legend of an apostolic foundation by Joseph of Arimathea, provided an answer of sorts, but the reliability of this entire history was being called into question by humanist scholars. Additional evidence with a firmer historical base was demanded if it was to be argued persuasively that the reformed church did not represent a radical discontinuity with the past history of English Christianity. Despite the efforts of successive medieval kings to limit papal authority, the essentially Roman character of the English church in post-Norman times was too evident to be disputed. However, it was hoped that a conscientious review of the church in earlier times would reveal a far more autonomous institution. Somewhat as the defenders of parliament against the king in the next century would move back to Saxon England to locate the roots of their freedoms, so the early English reformers hoped to find a more independent and purer church in a pre-Hildebrandian and pre-Norman era. This in effect meant Saxon times since, apart from a sketchy sixth-century history by Gildas, scant records of pre-Saxon England existed.

The dissolution of the monasteries and the subsequent dispersal of their great libraries made available to the enterprising scholar a vast collection of hitherto little-known historical materials.[3] Especially during the early Elizabethan years these records became the principal source of documentary material for antiquarians seeking to establish the legitimacy of the new ecclesiastical settlement.

One of the pioneers in the antiquarian search for a non-Roman church was John Bale, the passionate Protestant bishop and reformer. Rebelling against his monastic past, Bale repudiated everything Roman. Though in his early years he was opposed to the new humanist learning, he was widely read and deeply interested in history. Bitterly hostile to the monastic world of which he had once been a prominent member, he was nevertheless better aware than almost any other Englishman of the value of the library holdings that were being so carelessly dispersed and often wantonly destroyed. Following the lead of his friend John Leland, he urged authorities to give more attention to the valuable resources that were being lost to the nation. "What may brynge our realme to more shame and rebuke," he complained in 1549, "than to have it noysed abroade, that we are despysers of learnynge."[4] In an attempt to rescue monastic manuscripts he used his limited resources to purchase what he could and built up an impressive personal library collection. In a revealing letter to Archbishop Parker he explained the source of many of his books: "Some I found in stayconers and boke bynders store howses, some in grosers, sopesellars, taylers, and other occuyers shoppes, some in shyppes ready to be carryed over the sea into Flaunders to be solde—for in those uncircumspect and carelesse dayes, there was no quyckar merchaundyce than lybrary bokes, and all to destruction of learnynge and knowledge of thyngs necessary in thys fall of antichriste to be known[5]—but the devyll is a knave, they say—well, only conscyence, with a fervent love to my contray moved me to save what myghte be saved."[6] In 1552 Bale went to Ireland as Bishop of Ossory, bringing with him what was now a substantial library. But within a year following the restoration of Roman Catholicism under Mary, Bale precipitously sailed from Ireland leaving behind his great library. Its ultimate fate remains a mystery. One important fruit of Bale's bibliomania was the compilation of a chronlogical catalogue of English writers, which was later extended to form a rudimentary history of English literature.[7] In completing the catalogue he drew heavily on the work of Leland.

In the controversy with the Romanists over the character of

the true church—a controversy which helps explain the beginnings of Anglo-Saxon studies—no one played a more important role than Bale. In his most famous polemical work, *The Image of Both Churches,* he contrasted the purity of the true Christian church with the false church of Antichrist, "the sinful synagogue of satan."[8] Drawing on the mystical prophecies of the Book of Revelations, he portrayed the history of the church as one of a predestined decline from an original purity. The early popes were simple and poor men, modest in their aspirations; but after Constantine they grew preoccupied with worldly power and gradually became the agents of Satan.[9] From the year 1000—the year of the Antichrist foretold by St. John—the Church, under popes like Sylvester II and Gregory VII, suffered its greatest corruption. But the decline had been reversed; the reform movement, beginning with Wyclif, represented a return to original purity and the defeat of Antichrist "with all his hypocrisy disclosed."[10]

Reviewing the history of the English church, Bale stressed its early origins through its foundation by Joseph of Arimathea. This primitive church "which never had the authority of the Romish pope," continued until the papal mission of St. Augustine in 596.[11] Augustine supported by "Romish monks of Benets' superstition" was responsible for introducing practices and doctrines contrary to the spirit of Christ.[12] They came well armed "with Aristotles Artylerye, as with logyck, Philosophye, and other crafty scyences, but of the sacred scriptures, they knew lyttle or nothynge."[13] After the decisive year 1000, according to Bale, men like Anselm and Lanfranc introduced novel Hildebrandian policies and in consequence became involved in conflicts with the monarchy over temporal power as well as insisting on false practices and doctrines like clerical celibacy and transubstantiation.

Bale's writings, in spite of their intemperate quality, were important in proposing a line of defense for the new ecclesiastical settlement against Roman Catholic critics: the English Church was initially independent from Rome and remained more faithful than any other to the spirit of Christ; the introduction of Roman forms by St. Augustine began a period of decline which accelerated rapidly from the time of Hildebrand; the reform movement beginning with Wyclif and reaching its climax in the sixteenth century stood for a restoration of primitive purity and thus continuity with the early church. In this line of argument the history of the English church prior to the papal mission of Augustine might seem to be of decisive importance. However, given the paucity of records of the earlier period, the debate perforce came to focus on the pre-Hildebrandian or Saxon period.

No one worked more assiduously to bring to light the riches of early historical records than Bale's friend and collaborator John Leland. As royal chaplain and "king's antiquary" he was commissioned in 1533 to search after "England's antiquities, and peruse the libraries of all cathedrals, abbies, priories, colleges, etc. as also all places wherein records, writings, and secrets of Antiquity were reported."[14] For six years he scoured the country for material which he anticipated would lead him to the production of a great history—fifty volumes was his expressed goal—of the English nation, perhaps to be entitled *De nobilitate Britannica.* In addition to libraries, he studied and made extensive notes on Roman, Saxon and Danish remains. Though excessive preoccupation with a defense of the Arthurian legend against Polydore Vergil and an eventual drift into insanity prevented the completion of the planned history, the records and notes he left behind proved invaluable to later antiquarians.

Leland's motives were mixed. Like Bale he saw himself as a defender of the reformed church. A stated object of his work was "that the holy scryptures of God myghte both be sincerely taught and learned, all manner of superstycon, and crafty coloured doctryne of a rowte of Romayne Byshoppes, totally expelled oute of thys your most Catholyque realme."[15] In addition, a developing sense of national pride moved Leland to work so diligently at recovering the past. By efforts such as his own he believed a refutation would be forthcoming of those who judged the English nation a barbarous one. He was confident that the English realm "shall so well be knowne, ones paynted with hys natyre colours, that the renoume thereof shall geue place to the glory of no other regyon."[16]

The early Elizabethan years were decisive in settling the formal religious character of the English nation. In the work of building a national faith no one made a more substantial contribution than the martyrologist John Foxe. Like his mentor John Bale he was forced into exile during the Marian persecution, first to Frankfort and then Basle, where along with other English Protestants he brooded over the fate of the English church. Even before the accession of the Catholic Mary he had begun work on the book that was to establish his fame for centuries to come: *Actes and Monuments*, or as it was popularly known from its first appearance in 1563, *The Book of Martyrs*. In fact, Foxe's *Book* was far more than an account of Protestant martyrs; it was also a summary of the history of the Christian church from its inception, with special reference to the English church, and for generations it served as a principal source of English history for the general reader.

Following Bale, Foxe divided Church history into five divisions of roughly three hundred years each. The first 300 years witnessed the growth of the primitive or suffering church; the second was a period of relative calm with growing social influence; the third, from about the year 600, was marked by the increased claims of the papacy to spiritual and temporal power, the spread of monasticism, and the rise of Mohammedanism. In this third period the papal mission of Augustine to England and the conversion of the Saxons took place. It was characterized by a gradual decline that became more pronounced during the fourth period, especially after the year 1000, which saw the coming of Antichrist and the loosing of Satan. The work of Satan was well represented by Hildebrand who, as Pope Gregory VII, imposed clerical celibacy, controlled the appointments of bishops and even sought to place emperors under his jurisdiction. It was through Hildebrand "the sorcerer . . . that all this ambitious stoutness and pride entered first into the Church of Rome, and hath ever since continued."[17] The Norman rule imposed by William the Conqueror supported the triumph of Pope Gregory and excluded Englishmen to such an extent that "in his [William's] day there was almost no Englishman that bore office of honour or rule in the land. Insomuch that it was a half a shame at that time to be called an Englishman."[18] The final period was one of reform and return to the true Church of Christ, a movement begun by Wyclif and still in progress.

In commending English kings Foxe singled out Alfred. Above all others, he was a king of whom all Englishmen could be proud: "Among the Saxon kings . . . I find few or none to be preferred (or almost to be compared) to this Alured, or Alfred, for the great and singular qualities in this king, worthy of high renown and commendation–godly and excellent virtues, joined with a public and tender care, and a zealous study for the common peace and tranquillity or the weal public . . . his heroical properties joined together in one prince, as it is a thing most rare."[19] In Foxe's account of King Alfred, Englishmen at last had a worthy Saxon hero to replace the fabulous Arthur.

The hostility of the Normans to native English values, the impiety of the Roman church after Hildebrand, the monumental qualities of the Saxon Alfred, were important lessons to be drawn from Foxe's *Book* and, in time, were duly absorbed by most literate Englishmen to become essential ingredients of the developing national myth.

The anti-French bias which was a feature of the new-found pride in Saxon origins was well demonstrated by the attitude of John Aylmer, Marian exile and, later under Elizabeth, bishop of London. Writing from Switzerland in 1556 he berated the "effeminate Frenchmen: Stoute in bragge, but nothing in deede." Their contribution to English culture he dismissed as paltry: "We have a few hunting termes and pedlars French in the louyse lawe, brought in by the Normans, yet remanyning: But the language and customes bee Englyshe and Saxonyshe."[20]

Bale, Leland and especially Foxe had demonstrated in their attacks on Roman beliefs and practices how effectively medieval documents, especially of Saxon times, could be used as polemical weapons. The lesson was not lost on other English antiquaries. None turned it to better advantage than Matthew Parker, the first Elizabethan Archbishop of Canterbury. Parker was consecrated Archbishop in December 1559. A moderate Protestant, he was charged with the responsibility of maintaining and justifying an 'Ecclesia Anglicana' lying somewhere between Puritanism and Roman Catholicism, with broad enough appeal to hold the allegiance of the majority of Englishmen. As a theologian and scholar thoroughly familiar with Reformation controversy, he recognized that a convincing justification of the Elizabethan church settlement depended on a clear demonstration that it represented a continuity with the church that existed in Saxon times, a period when, it had to be shown, papal claims were not yet fully developed. In particular it must be shown that doctrines and practices such as papal supremacy, clerical celibacy, latin liturgy, and transubstantiation were late innovations. Assertions by Bale and Foxe that the Saxon church was far closer to the purity of the primitive church than was the case in post-Norman times had to be more carefully substantiated. To popularize this it was necessary to make better known appropriate Anglo-Saxon writings as well as a selection of those of later writers, like Matthew Paris, who were known to be hostile to the papacy and could help illumine the earlier period. Parker's task was complicated by the fact that the single great history from Saxon times, Bede's *Historia Ecclesiastica*, was thoroughly Roman in inspiration. (The able Catholic controversialist Thomas Stapleton who edited the *Historia* in 1565 dedicated it to the Queen to show her "in what faithe your noble Realme was christened, and hath almost these thousand yeres contineuued.")[21]

Within a few months after his consecration Parker was in correspondence with John Bale concerning the recovery of books and manuscripts dispersed during the rape of the monastic libraries.[22] With the able assistance of his Latin secretary, John Joscelyn, he set about collecting what became an impressive collection of ancient English historical records. With other former

Cambridge men like Alexander Neville and George Acworth, his household became a center for antiquarian studies. In providing the resources and direction for this work, Parker, more than any person was responsible for the revival of interest in the Anglo-Saxon language and culture, and he merits the title conferred on him by his biographer as "the chief Retriever of that our ancient Native Language."[23]

The first work that issued from Parker's group in 1556 was a selection from the writings of an eleventh-century Saxon abbot, Aeelfric. Its title clearly indicates the ecclesiastical motive behind its printing: *a Testimonie of Antiquitie, shewing the auncient fayth in the Church of England touching the sacrament of the body and bloude of the Lord here publikely preached, and also recaued in the Saxons tyme, above 600 yeares agoe*. Printed in Saxon and English, it introduced readers to what for most of them must have been a totally unfamiliar language. The next year Joscelyn edited Gildas's *Britanniae*, a sixth-century Latin history of the Roman and Anglo-Saxon conquests. Gildas's history, notable for the absence of any mention of King Arthur, had been published by Polydore Vergil in 1525, but his work was judged unsatisfactory. As the only book of its kind written in England in the sixth century, it was regarded as of unique importance.

In 1571, under Parker's prompting and Joscelyn's editorial assistance, an edition of the Anglo-Saxon texts of the Gospels was produced.[24] Though Foxe's knowledge of Anglo-Saxon was almost certainly slight, editorship was assigned to him, undoubtedly to take advantage of his established reputation.[25] Foxe noted in his preface that nothing was more needful "then the opening to this our age the tymes of old antiquities." The printing of the Gospels in the ancient language was seen as of special significance: "Imprinted thus in the Saxone letters [it] may remaine in the Church as a profitable example and president of old antiquitie . . . how the religion presently taught and professed in the Church at thys present, is no new reformation of thinges lately begonne, which were not before, but rather a reduction of the Church to the Pristine state of olde conformitie." It should furthermore prove how much in error were those who "judged our native tounge unmeete to expresse God's high secret mysteries, being so barbarous and imperfecte a language."[26]

The year following the publication of the Saxon gospels the only major historical work written (or at least fostered) by Parker appeared: *De Antiquitate Britannicae Ecclesiae*. Its object was in Parker's words, "to note at what time Augustine my first predecessor came into this land, what religion he brought in with him, and how it continued."[27] Parker predictably rejected the claim of Augustine as founder of English Christianity, referring its beginnings to Joseph of Arimathea. In 1574 he published an edition of Bishop Asser's tenth-century *Life of King Alfred* (*De Rebus Gesti Aeelfredi Magni*). Printed in Latin but in old English characters–*lingua Latina, sed literis Saxonicis*–the edition was prefaced with a strong plea by Parker on behalf of the Anglo-Saxon language, stressing its utility not only to theologians but also to men of affairs.

Though by modern standards of scholarship Parker was extremely careless in his editorial work, frequently altering words and making unacknowledged additions to the text, his service to the promotion of a greater sympathy and understanding of a previously little known period was invaluable. He was responsible for the preservation of a wealth of early historical material. Among the Parker manuscripts at Corpus Christi, Cambridge, which received a large part of his collection, are thirty-eight in Old English, indicating the magnitude of his efforts to illuminate Saxon England. While the primary motive behind his labors was always to defend the Elizabethan church settlement, he was a genuine English patriot and scholar who wished to promote a greater knowledge of the past achievements of a people on the way to national greatness.[28]

The work of promoting interest in England's antiquities was by no means restricted to Parker's group. William Cecil, Lord Burghley, from his earliest Cambridge years was interested in historical scholarship, an interest which continued when he became the most powerful statesman of the realm under Elizabeth. He maintained an extensive library and rivaled Parker in his collection of ancient books and manuscripts. As a principal architect of Elizabethan political policy, he found a more exact knowledge of England's history and geography a distinct asset. Thus he was prepared to support those who manifested an interest in recovering ancient records.

Cecil's protégé, Laurence Nowell, Dean of Lichfield became one of the most enthusiastic Saxonists of his day.[29] He lived in Cecil's home while tutor to his ward, the Earl of Oxford. There he made transcripts of early manuscripts, including an Anglo-Saxon translation of Bede, the Anglo-Saxon Chronicles, and a collection of Saxon laws that proved invaluable to later scholars. Nowell compiled the first Anglo-Saxon dictionary, *Vocabularium Saxonium*, and though not published, it was available to later antiquaries. His pupil, William Lambarde, a member of Lincoln's Inn, was particularly interested in early English law. His first work, published in 1568 with the encouragement of Nowell, was a collection of Anglo-Saxon laws, the *Archaionomia*. Though only a fragmentary collection and poorly translated, it was highly valued as a law textbook and remained the only collection of Old English laws for a century.[30] The question of the continuity of English law would of course become of critical importance in the heated seventeenth century debates over royal supremacy.

In 1576, drawing extensively on Old English documents, Lambarde published the first county history—*A Perambulation of Kent*. He became Master of the Rolls in 1594 and Lord Keeper in 1596. His conscientious work in bringing to light and preserving ancient records, and especially those dealing with the antiquity of English law, prompted the Queen's gracious, "Farewell, good and honest Lambarde," on the occasion of an audience granted to him a few weeks before his death.[31]

Lambarde's concentration on legal records represents a moving away from the ecclesiastical disputes that had so occupied men like Leland, Bale, Foxe and Parker. By the time of Parker's death in 1575 the Elizabethan Church settlement (much aided by Pius V's ill-fated bull *Regnans in Excelsis*) had taken firm root. More and more, antiquarian interest broadened to embrace pressing political and constitutional issues. The preoccupation of the Society of Antiquaries, founded around 1586, demonstrates this. So political was its orientation that it came to be viewed with the greatest distrust by James I and it was finally disbanded, as a result of royal disfavor, in 1614. Members of the Society, even more than the earlier antiquaries, stressed the importance of the Saxon element in English history. Of a more secular cast of mind than their predecessors, they were far more influenced by the humanistic currents of the Renaissance with its exaltation of antiquity. Pride in the past came to be rooted as much in racial and national considerations as in religious. In this movement the influence of German humanism deserves special notice.

German humanists believed that their glorious past had been ignored and slighted by most of the ancient writers as well as by contemporary Italian scholars. It was their self-appointed task to resurrect their history and demonstrate that it was as venerable and worthy of esteem as that of the Greeks or Romans. Furthermore they would show that the Germany of antiquity lived on to flower in their own day. In this enterprise the great humanist poet Konrad Celtis (1459-1508) led the way. A passionate nationalist, he extolled the greatness of Germany, past and present. He encouraged its scholars to delve into their past to uncover its riches and make the German people conscious of their proud heritage. Celtis's plea struck a responsive chord in a host of scholars throughout the Germanic lands. The history of the Teutonic peoples was studied and commented upon with their widespread migrations presented as proof of their superior qualities. The excellence of the German language became a common theme of philologists and a cult of its purity developed. In 1518 an Alsatian doctor, Lorenz Fries, argued the superiority of German over French on the grounds that the former was an original language while the latter was "collected together by begging from the Greeks and Latins, from the Goths and the Huns."[32] A more extravagant defender of the German language was the Flemish physician, Joannes Becanus (1518-1572). He claimed German as the language of the Garden of Eden as well as the original language of the Old Testament. All other modern languages save German, in his view, took their origins from the Tower of Babel and were marked with inferiority.[33]

In the work of creating a new pride of race, no text was held in higher esteem than Tacitus's essay *On the Origin and Geography of Germany*. Writing in 98 B.C., Tacitus contrasted the virtue of the Germans with the degeneracy of the Empire. "For myself," he wrote in a famous passage, "I accept the view that the peoples of Germany have never been tainted by intermarriage with other peoples, and stand out as a nation peculiar, pure and unique of its kind."[34] Celtis brought out an edition of the *Germania* in 1500 and it quickly became a primary document for all subsequent advocates of German racial superiority. (Modern scholars discount the *Germania* as an inadequate account of early Germanic society.)[35]

A leading spokesman for the rising German consciousness was Ulrich von Hutten (1488-1523). He dreamed of a new united Germany freed from papal influence and the pretensions of princes. His translation of Lorenzo Valla's work exposing as a forgery the famous Donation of Constantine prompted an English translation at the height of the Henrician reformation. Von Hutten contrasted the virtues and virility of the German people with the femininity of the Romano-Welsche: "A woman race. . . . These are the people who rule us! This mockery breaks my heart."[36] The image of a virtuous and manly Germany held back and tyrannized by Latin enemies became a recurring theme among German nationalists.

As Renaissance humanism gave way to the fury of the Reformation, Martin Luther emerged as the most strident defender of German identity. With a voice eventually heard throughout Europe, he protested that though the second Roman empire was built on German foundations its fruits were gathered by others: "We have the title of empire, but the pope has our goods, our honour, our bodies, lives, souls and all we possess. That is the way to cheat the Germans, and because they are Germans, to go on cheating them."[37] Luther called upon the ruling class of the German people to end the age-old exploitation of the German *nation* and unwittingly gave a powerful impetus to the growth of secular nationalism. As a devout Christian he accepted the biblical account of the origins of man, but saw the Germans as first by right of their descent from Ashkenaz, first-born of Gomer, who through first-born descent from Japheth and Noe led back to Adam, the father of the human race. Like other nationalists Luther stressed the invaluable instrument the Germans possessed in their language: "I thank God that I am able to hear and find my God in the German language, whom neither I nor you would ever find in Latin or Greek or Hebrew."[38]

Out of the Renaissance and the Reformation a myth developed of an orginal Germanic people with roots reaching back to Adam, possessing a language and culture richer than and independent from any other. In this myth the Germanic achievement was everything and the contributions of other peoples, whether classical or medieval, irrelevant. As the persecuted Germanic people wrested European hegemony from the Romans by virtue of their might, so the Reformation represented a sweeping away by Germans of the false pretensions of Latin Christianity. History demonstrated that Germany was great in and through itself.

German influence in England was at first most apparent in religious affairs. From the beginning English reformers turned to German religious leaders for inspiration and support. A leading German reformer Martin Bucer, for example, was consulted by Henry VIII on his divorce, advised religious leaders like Cranmer and Parker, and was eventually appointed as Regius Professor of divinity at Cambridge. London was a favorite place of refuge for German Protestants, as Strasbourg became a well-known center for English religious exiles.

While the frequent discussions between German and English reformers confirmed a common religious bond, slight attention was initially given to the question of a common ancestry. This awaited the calming of religious passions and the growth of a greater concern with secular national issues. Also, an interpretation of the past derived from Geoffrey's *History of the Kings of Britain* still prevailed and satisfied most Englishmen. Leland, Bale, Parker and their associates, in spite of their important contribution to the revival of interest in the Anglo-Saxon past, were loath to abandon a version of history which could be readily adapted to support a national church and whose main critic was an Italian papist, Polydore Vergil. Until the late Elizabethan era there were few enthusiasts for race theories lauding Germanic origins and Saxon superiority. Writing in 1593, Richard Harvey, a Cambridge champion of the Trojan origin of the British people, felt no compunction in omitting entirely from his defense of the Brut any account of the Saxons: "What have I to do with them unless it were to make them tributary to Brutans . . . Let them lie in dead forgetfulness like stones."[39]

William Camden (1551-1623) was the first English scholar to give detailed attention to the historic origins of the Anglo-Saxons. More than any of his contemporaries he was influenced by continental historical scholarship and was quite familiar with the work of contemporary German and Italian humanists. Around 1580, together with a small group of Oxford academics, Camden began to pursue readings of Italian historians. Tacitus was a favorite author. He maintained a fairly extensive correspondence with his friend, Thomas Savile, and his brother, the erudite Sir Henry Savile, the English translator of Tacitus.

At the urging of the Dutch geographer Abraham Ortelius, Camden undertook the work that was to establish his fame, the *Britannia* (1586). In addition to European historians, both classical and modern, and standard British authorities such as Gildas and Bede, he drew extensively on the work of Leland and Lambarde. To complete his history he found he had to acquire a knowledge not only of Saxon but also of the ancient British tongue. The bulk of his *Britannia* was an account of Britain between the coming of the Saxons and the advent of the Normans. Drawing upon topography and geography as well as history, Camden presented his work as a "Chorographical description" of the British Isles. In the preface he clearly stated what motivated his work: "a common love for our country, and the glory of the British name."[40] Religious polemic was given little place in Camden's narrative.

Though Camden was sensitive to the attachment of many Englishmen to Geoffrey's *History*, he was inclined to treat the account as entirely irrelevant, for it was "of little authority among learned men." In the section of his *Britannia* dealing with "The English-Saxons," he was at pains to emphasize their Germanic origin. His praise of their courage and valor echoes Tacitus. He saw their victory over the native inhabitants of England "entire and absolute": "All the conquered, except a few who took refuge in the uncultivated western parts, yielded and became one nation with them, and embraced their laws, name, and language; for, besides, England, the English-Saxons possessed themselves of the greatest part of Scotland . . . where they use the same language with us, only varying a little in the dialect, and his language we and they have kept in a manner uncorrupted together with the kingdom, for 1150 years."[41] Anglo-Saxonism had at last a worthy spokesman.

In a miscellaneous collection of notes entitled *Remaines Concerning Britain* (1605), Camden was fulsome in his praise of the Germans and acknowledged the debt the English people owed them for their nation and language: "This English tongue is extracted, as the nations, from the Germans, the most glorious of all now extant in Europe for their morall, and martiall vertues, and preserving the liberty entire, as also for propagating their language by happie victories in France by the Francs, and Burgundians; in this Isle by the English-Saxons; in Italy by the Heruli, West-Goths, Vandals, and Lombards; in Spain by the Suevians and Vandales." Camden, as much as any of his language-conscious Renaissance contemporaries, saw the greatness of the Saxons—"This warlike, victorious, stiff, stout and vigorous nation"—manifested in the development of their language: "Our English tongue is (I will not say as sacred as the Hebrew, or as learned as the Greek) but as fluent as the Latin, as courteous as the Spanish, as courtlike as the French, and as amorous as the Italian." The martial vigor of the Saxons was matched by their acknowledged spiritual achievements: "As for abroad, the world can testify that four Englishmen have converted to Christianitie eight Nations of Europe [viz. Boniface, Willebrod, Nicholas Brakespeare, Thomas de Walden]. . . . Neither will I here note, which strangers have observed, that England hath bred more Princes renowned for sanctitie, than any Christian nation whatsoever."[42] Even the movements of the heavens favored the Saxons, for, of Northern origin, they came under that special influence of Jupiter and Mars which made them "impatient of servitude, lovers of liberty, martiall and courageous."[43]

An even stauncher advocate of Germanic superiority and Saxon virtue was Richard Verstegen. His family name was Rowlands, but pride in his German ancestry led him to assume the name of his grandfather. While a student at Oxford he became interested in early English history and acquired a knowledge of Anglo-Saxon. A zealous Catholic, he declined to undergo the compulsory religious tests and left Oxford without a degree. In 1605 he published his most important work: *Restitution of Decayed Intelligence.* He professed to demonstrate in his work, "what a highly renowned and most honourable Nation the *Germans* have always been, that thereby it may consequently appear how honourable it is for *English-men* to be from them descended."[44] Verstegen boldly dedicated his work to King James, "the chiefest Blood-Royal of our ancient English-Saxon Kings," and thus set aside the Stuart claim to British ancestry and James's vision of himself as a second Arthur.

Verstegen's book was a panegyric to the Germanic descent of the English. The German nation was "the Tree from which *English men,* as a most stately and flourishing branch, are issued and sprung forth." Its greatness and purity was attested to by Tacitus. Its line of descent, direct and unpolluted, went back to Japhet. The Germans were worthy of renown and glory for three principal reasons: (1) no people had ever inhabited Germany save the Germans themselves; (2) they had never been subdued; (3) they had neither mixed with foreign people nor had their language ever been mixed with a foreign tongue. Given these points "of greatest National Honour," Verstegen doubted "whether any People else in the World can challenge to have equality with them."[45]

Verstegen was one of the first antiquarians to confront the question which was to prove so bothersome to later Anglo-Saxonists: did not the Danish, and more particularly the Norman conquests substantially alter the Saxon character of England? Verstegen responded in two ways. First, he minimized their significance. The number of Danes and Normans who ultimately remained were, in his mind, very few in respect to the English: "The main Corps and Body of the Realm, notwithstanding the *Norman* Conquest, and the former Invasions of the *Danes,* hath still consisted of the ancient *English-Saxon* people, wherein even unto this day it doth yet consist." For the unconvinced he had another argument: "And whereas some do call us a mixed Nation by reason of these *Danes* and *Normans* coming in among us. I answer (as formerly I have noted) that the *Danes* and the *Normans* were once one same people with the *Germans,* as were also the Saxons; and we are not to be accompted mixed by having only some such joined unto us again, as sometime had one same language, and one same original with us."[46]

In a discussion of the great antiquity of the English tongue, Verstegen hesitated to go as far as his friend Abraham Ortelius who, following Becanus, held the Teutonic tongue to be the original language of Adam. For Verstegen it was sufficient, "that if the Teutonick be not taken for the first Language of the World, it cannot be denied to be one of the most ancientest of the World." It maintained, in Verstegen's opinion, a purity which was lost to Italian, Spanish and French.[47]

Despite their acknowledged Germanic ancestry, Verstegen discounted the contribution of the Normans to the development of the English language. He undoubtedly would have supported Camden's proud boast, "that the olde *English* could express most aptly, all the conceiptes of the minde in their owne tongue without borrowing from any,"[48] and echoed the gratitude of the dedicated Saxonist, William L'Isle, who thanked God "that he that conquered the Land could not so conquer the language."[49] Equally, he would have agreed with the sentiments of the Germanophile Alexander Gil who wrote in 1619: "O you English, you I appeal to in whose veins flows that ancestral blood; retain, retain what hitherto remains of your native tongue, and follow in the footprints of your ancestors."[50]

Verstegen's work ran to five editions by 1673. Though sometimes casually dismissed as an "odd" or "curious" book, it represents the first comprehensive presentation in English of a theory of national origin based on a belief in the racial superiority of the Germanic people, a theme repeated a thousand times in succeeding centuries.

In spite of appearance, in their idealization of the past the Saxonists were not turning their back on the new England. They were deeply imbued with nationalistic sentiments and saw England's future as one of progress and expansion. William L'Isle was representative. In his eloquent call for a revived sense of the greatness of the German family, he struck almost an imperial note: "But rise-up (O!) some one to our kingdome, more therewith commanding then ever King did; more learned than ever King was; and after so many cruell warres betwixt the Britons and Saxons (the heire to them both) looke backe againe to the place, from whence we the latter, but more victorious and happy came; remember that, whom you now entitle the Emperor of Germany, he was in our time called the Keasor of Saxland; as indeed of our Nation that huge continent was peopled and named. O love thou then the Emperiall Families thereof, howsoever discording among themselves: for thou shalt have power to make peace and prove the *Salomon* of this latter age."[51]

As tension between crown and parliament steadily intensified in the early decades of the seventeenth century, the Saxon antiquarians found that their interests were not irrelevant to the great issues of the day. Those set on changing the structures of English society, from the beginning understood that their cause would be greatly strengthened if it was perceived as a defense of historic rights against an innovating crown. The historical investigation of Anglo-Saxon England took on a new urgency. A study that had arisen in the sixteenth century in response to a *religious* need was found in the seventeenth to serve the highest *political* purposes.

Chapter III

ENGLISH ANTIQUITY

Parliament's Good Servant

James I, allegedly of the line of Brut and a new Arthur preordained to unite the two kingdoms of England and Scotland, was compelled by temperament and circumstances to stand against irresistible currents that were to change the face of English society. From at least the last decade of Elizabeth's reign it was evident that the alliance between crown and parliament that had served both institutions so well was under severe strain. With the elimination of factors which had once threatened the unity of the nation—the Spanish menace, papal influence in church affairs, fractious nobles—the interests of the landholders and the men of business, the principal groups represented in parliament, no longer coincided completely with the interests of the crown. Parliament had reached a stage in its development when it was not prepared to accept passively royal policy. For its part, the crown, with ever growing expenses was anxious to gain a share of the rapidly increasing commercial wealth. While Elizabeth lived, parliamentary pressures were kept within limits. But upon her death, despite the enthusiastic welcome given to James, parliament was determined to have its way.

It was both the strength and misfortune of King James and his ill-fated son to be identified with forces that stood solidly for the maintenance of the old England: a nobility dependent upon royal support and a church hierarchy that over the previous century had become an arm of royal policy. The Laudian church in particular, was viewed by its Puritan critics as fostering a kind of Arminianism that promoted the worst features of papalism and, by many who had no sympathy for Puritan religious dogma, it was seen as an organization that stood in the way of economic progress. The monarchy on the other hand, with its evident Catholic sympathies at home and its overtures to France and Spain abroad, seemed to be deliberately pursuing a policy directly against the expectations of the majority of Englishmen. From the outbreak of the Thirty Years' War it appeared to many parliamentarians that the crown had allied itself with the forces of the Counter Reformation in a conspiracy to snuff out Protestantism. James I could boast of at least a relative success in withstanding parliamentary pressures, but the seeds of discontent so evident throughout his reign were to produce a harvest to be reaped in full by his son. Charles I may be criticized for intransigence and an exaggerated advocacy of the royal prerogative, but it is doubtful if anything short of revolution would have satisfied those set on radical change.

Opposition to the Stuart policy came naturally to be centered in parliament, for it was there that the commercial interests and land holders had their only national forum. The doctrine of the Divine Right of Kings as such was not an issue; few apart from a small group of radicals questioned it in theory. King, parliament, and common lawyers alike accepted the theory of a balanced constitution derived from inalienable rights possessed by crown and subjects and interpreted according to common law. However, there were a variety of opinions on how the constitution should be worked out in practice. The failure of the early Stuart monarchs lay in their inability to grasp the dynamic nature of the English compromise that enabled a monarch to assert supremacy in both state and church and at the same time to admit a legitimate sharing of authority.

James I himself was to a considerable measure responsible for determining that the debate would turn on the historic origin of respective rights. Even before coming to London, he maintained that by virtue of the Norman Conquest the English monarch was absolute owner of all property within the kingdom, an argument scarcely calculated to win support from a property-conscious middle class. Once installed, his inflexible stand on regal rights did little to placate suspicious subjects set on political reform.

From the very beginning those seeking to limit the royal prerogative perceived the value of antiquarian studies. The lessons of the sixteenth-century religious controversies were not lost on them. As an appeal to the Saxon past had been useful to those anxious to upset the traditional religious establishment, so it was to prove to reformers seeking to alter constitutional arrangements. Thus, in its appeal to antiquity for validation, a movement which was essentially modern and progressive took on a curiously anachronistic appearance.

Since the death of Archbishop Parker antiquarian interest had shifted from religious to political concerns. When the Society of Antiquaries was founded in the 1580s questions related to constitutional issues dominated its discussions. Its membership included not only those regarded as professional antiquarians, but active politicians like William Cecil who had ready access to State papers. In the early years of the seventeenth century, however, the Society suffered a decline and its original membership dispersed.

James had early perceived the danger of an alliance between antiquarians and the parliamentary opposition led by the common lawyers. Topics of common interest to both antiquarians and parliamentarians, such as the Saxon origin of parliament and the continuity of English laws and customs, raised questions that were politically charged. When Henry Spelman (later the editor of *Archaeologus*, a glossary of Saxon and Latin law terms, and the founder of an Anglo-Saxon lectureship at Cambridge), along with other prominent scholars like Camden and Robert Cotton, sought to revive the Society in 1614, in spite of a promise to avoid controversial discussion, the king showed his disfavor. Spelman put the best interpretation he could on the king's opposition, explaining that the king took "a little Mislike of our Society, not being inform'd that we had resolv'd to decline all Matters of State."[1] In the event only a single meeting was held. James's distrust, however, did little to divert a growing interest among antiquarians in placing the origins of English liberties in Saxon days, a time when the king, allegedly chosen by the people, served primarily as a *dux bellorum*. No one had higher praise for the virtues and governmental skills of the Saxons—"a Nation fierce and valorous"—than the historian John Speed. In his *History of Great Britaine* (1614) he extolled the "Manhood" of the Saxons, who of all the Germans "were accounted the best for courage of minde, strength of body, and enduring of trauell." (The manly qualities of the Saxons becomes a recurring theme among Saxon enthusiasts).

Speed outlined the Saxon system of choosing their governors as one that severely limited the power of the king: "For the generall gouernment of their Countrey they ordayned twelve Noblemen chosen from among others, for their worthiness and sufficiency . . . but ever in time of warre one of these twelve was chosen to be King, and so to remaine so long onely as the warres lasted: and that being ended, his name and dignitie of *King* also ceased, becoming againe as before. And this custome continued among them, until the wars with the *Emperor Charles the Great*."[2]

Those who favored severely limiting royal authority stressed the antiquity of parliament and thereby suggested that its authority was prior and superior to that of kings. Initially the defense of parliament's immemorial origins was led by the common lawyers, who, for their own advantage, sought to restrict the royal prerogative. As interest grew in establishing a specifically national origin for the institution of parliament, arguments in favor of its Germanic or Gothic (as it came to be called in the seventeenth century) origins came to the fore.

As the century developed, the association between antiquarian researchers and parliamentary opposition continued to grow. By the end of James I's reign, scholars and politicians like Selden, Coke, Eliot, Wentworth, Pym will be found meeting at the home of Sir John Cotton to discuss matters of pressing political concern.[3] Defense of parliament as the cornerstone of English freedoms was of high priority. Within parliament itself Sir Edward Coke emerged as the stoutest champion for its antiquity. He took the arguments of the antiquarians and pushed them to the breaking point: parliament as an institution long ante-dated Henry I, who was its restorer not its originator. Parliament, according to Coke, was to be identified with the Saxon witenagemot or even the British *Conventus* described by Tacitus.[4] Though the research of serious scholars like Selden and Cotton offered no support for Coke's extravagant views, they still gained popular support. It was Coke also who was primarily responsible for converting Magna Charta into a symbol of the free man inspired by his Saxon past standing against unlimited royal power. Coke first cited the charter in parliament in 1610, contending that it limited the king's power to alter ancient customs. From that date it came to be quoted in both parliament and the courts whenever the question of the supremacy of the law over the royal prerogative arose. In time, the charter came to be accepted as the basic law of a constitution reaching back to Saxon times which guaranteed the general liberties of Englishmen. As one commentator has written, the seventeenth-century history of Magna Charta "is a classic example of how a misinterpretation of the past may acquire an historical importance of its own."[5]

In documenting the case for the antiquity and continuity of English customs and institutions, commentators gave special importance to three medieval texts: *Modus Tenendi Parliamentum*, *Mirror of Justice* and *De Laudibus Legum Angliae*. The *Modus* was a fourteenth-century composition which purported to give a detailed account of parliamentary procedure during the reign of Edward the Confessor. Its aim as stated in the introduction left no doubt on the Saxon origin of parliament and its continuity in post-Conquest times. "Here is set out the method of holding the parliament of the king of England and of his English in the times of King Edward the son of King Ethelred: which method was recited by the more discreet of the realm in the presence of William, duke of Normandy, conqueror and king of England, on the orders of the conqueror himself, and approved by him, and used in his times and also in the times of his successors the kings of England."[6]

The Mirror of Justice, a thirteenth-century work, was written in French by Andrew Horn, "an ardent Teutonist who ignores the Norman Conquest."[7] The author traced the beginning of British law "to the coming of the English" and made it clear that from the earliest Saxon times the king was freely chosen by the people and ruled under carefully defined conditions: "They made him swear that he would maintain the Christian faith with all his power, and would guide his people by law without respect of any person, and would be obedient to holy Church, and would submit to justice and would suffer right like any other of his people." The primacy of parliament was guaranteed: "It was agreed as law that the king should have companions to hear and determine in the parliaments all the writs and plaints concerning wrongs done by the king, the queen, their children, and their special ministers, for which wrongs one could not otherwise have obtained common right." King Alfred himself ordained as "a perpetual usage" that parliament should assemble twice a year. Of the abuses that developed, the first and sovereign was that the king should be seen as beyond the law, "whereas he ought to be subject to it, as is contained in his oath"; the second was the infrequent calling of parliament (contrary to the rule that it should be held twice a year).[8]

Understandably the *Mirror of Justice* (still in manuscript form) was seized upon and popularized by Coke, who believed "that he had acquired a treatise which set forth the law of King Arthur's day."[9] It appropriately was first printed in 1642 with an edition appearing in English in 1646.

In the debates over the continuity of English laws and institutions, no work was cited more often by opponents to the royal policy than Sir John Fortescue's *De Laudibus Legum Angliae* (c. 1470). Fortescue asserted that the origin of the existing laws and customs of England reached back to the earliest beginnings of English society: "the realm has been continuously ruled by the same customs as it is at present." In Fortescue's judgment neither the laws of the Romans, nor the Venetians, nor "the Laws of any other Kingdom in the World are so venerable for their Antiquity." And he triumphantly concluded: "there's no Pretence to say, or insinuate to the contrary, but that the *Laws* and *Customs* of *England* are not only good, but the *very Best*."[10] The first English translation of Fortescue's work had appeared in 1567 and was popularly acclaimed. In 1616 John Selden brought out an annotated edition offering cautious but substantial criticism. In spite of Selden, however, Fortescue's notion of the immutable character of the English law and the continuity of its institutions, under the powerful advocacy of Coke, became a dogma of the parliamentary opposition. "There are plain footsteps of those Laws in the Government of the Saxons," proclaimed John Pym in a famous debate on the Petition of Rights in 1628.[11] As the parliamentary supporters went on to triumph in the Civil War, the Anglo-Saxon origins of English liberties became a confirmed ingredient of the new national myth.

As opposition to the policies of Charles I continued to grow, parliamentary leaders were regarded as "patriots," a term that came into currency in the seventeenth century to describe one who self-sacrificingly or disinterestedly defended the well-being of his country against king and court. Writing of John Hampden in 1640, Clarendon related: "The eyes of all men were fixed on him as their *Patriae pater*, and the pilot that must steer their vessel through the tempests and rocks which threatened it."[12] With the ultimate triumph of the parliamentarians, Anglo-Saxonism and patriotism were on the way to becoming interchangeable terms.

It was during the opening year of the Civil War that the most impassioned plea to date on behalf of Anglo-Saxonism poured from the pen of John Hare: *St. Edward's Ghost*. The extravagance of his racial rhetoric would not be equaled again until the nineteenth century. To Hare there was no doubt as to the lofty origin of Englishmen: "There is no man understands rightly what an English man is, but knows withall that we are a member of the Teutonick Nation, and descended out of Germany; a descent so honourable and happy (if duly considered) as like could not have been fetched from any other part of Europe, nor scarce of the universe, which will be plaine and manifest if we take a just survey of the gloriousness of that our Mother Nation. . . . To the Antiquity of the Teutonic house, there wants not a conspiring quality of blood effectual to make it the most illustrious and primer Nation of Christendome." It was a descent reaching back to Noe through Ashkenaz, his great grandson, and "the father and denominator of the German Nation."[13]

Englishmen, urged Hare, should glory in their German Ancestry and in the racial purity they, the most noble of the Germanic tribes, retained: "Such is the transcendent quality of our

Mother Nation, and in these sundry respects, she sufficiently appeares to be the cheife and most honourable Nation of Europe; of all which honours of her, we are the true inheritors and partakers, either as Member of that body or as children of that Mother, we being flesh of her flesh, and bone of her bone, yea of the most ancient and noble of her tribes (according to the Germanes opinion) . . . our Progenitors that transplanted themselves from Germany hither, did not commixe themselves with the ancient inhabitants of the Countrey the Britaines (as other Colonies did with the Natives in those places where they came) but totally expelling them, they took the sole possession of the Land to themselves, thereby preserving their blood, lawes, and language incorrupted . . . it is well knowne that most Colonies and transmigrators are made up and consisting of the floure and choice youth of that Country from whence they are transplanted." Englishmen could boast of an inheritance that not only gave them purity of blood but also provided them with superior laws and institutions: "Neither was this our generosity of blood and freeness of descent and condition, the summe of our inheritance as the whole stock of honour that the bounty of heaven had committed to our possession; we were also blest with a hopefull language and happy Lawes; Lawes envied but not equall'd in *Christendome*, and by historians admired as most plaine and compendious, and of such a political structure, as made our Prince a true and happy Monarch, and yet ourselves as free as any people of Europe." And in Saxon they possessed a language superior to Latin and its derivatives: "Our language was a dialect of the Teutonick, and although then but in her infancie, yet not so rude as hopefull, being most fruitfull and copious in significant and well-founding rootes and Primitives, and withall capable and apt for diffusion from those her rootes into such a Greek-like ramosity of derivations and compositions, beyond the power of the Latine and her off-spring dialects. . . ."[14]

To Hare it was intolerable that a nation of "so noble an extraction and descent" and with "such Priviledges conferred on us by heaven" should be so "un-Teutonized" as a result of the Norman

Conquest. That the Normans in the main might be considered a Germanic people was of small comfort, for they represented at best "the off-scouring, the drosse of the Teutonic and Gallic Nation." Like a true reformer, Hare outlined a program of action directed to the re-Teutonizing of England. It should begin with a repudiation of everything Norman. William, "sirnamed the Conqueror," should be "stript of that insolent title," and be either declared a usurper or be judged king "by force of St. Edward's legacy." Englishmen claiming Norman descent should "repudiate their names and titles brought over from Normandy" (they might even consider themselves Norwegians in order to shake off any "tincture of Gallicisme"). All laws and usages of Norman origin should be abolished and English laws "devested of their French rags . . . be restored into the English or Latine tongue." All French words should be purged from the language and replaced with words and terms "from the old Saxon and the learned tongues." If the above steps were taken, then pride of Anglo-Saxon race and nation would be restored and England's mission realized: "Then shall we with alacrity presse all that the English name investeth, unto the defence and inlargement of the English Dominion . . . we shall joy to make Anglicisme become the only soule and habit of all both *Ireland* and *Great Britaine*."[15]

In 1647, at a decisive period in the Civil War, a comprehensive study by Nathaniel Bacon outlining the Saxon origins of parliamentary privileges and their continuity in later history appeared. Bacon appealed to antiquity against the arbitrary claims of Monarchs. "A King amongst the Saxons," he observed, "in probability was anciently a Commander in the field, an Officer *pro tempore*, and no necessary member in the constitution of their state." In time he who was initially only a *dux bellorum* became *Rex*, but this did not alter his essentially dependent role: "he that formerly was a servant for the occasion, afterwards became a servant for life, yet clothed with Majesty, like some bitter Pill covered with Gold, to make the service better tasted." Thus "a Saxon king was no other than a *primum mobile* set in regular motion, by Lawes established by the whole body of the Kingdom."[16] Bacon's work was widely read in succeeding decades, running to six editions by 1760, and had a major influence in firmly fixing in the English mind an acknowledged association between current freedoms and the Saxon past.

The developing spirit of nationalism rooted in pride of race and language was likewise apparent in Francis Whyte's *For the Sacred Law of the Land* (1652). "But we live not only for ourselves," Whyte exhorted his readers in his opening salutation, "something we owe to mankind, more to our own blood, to our mother England." It was evident to Whyte that the English law—which is "Liberty itself"—was not derived from the Normans: "The fundamentals are Saxon-English." The ancient Saxon customs and liberties which make up the common law were restored by Alfred the Great and confirmed again in the time of John in the Great Charter. The fountain of English liberty was thus German rather than Norman. The Saxon tongue, the mother German tongue, was matchless, "in that it borrows lesse, and is more copious and significant then others."[17]

The vision of the Anglo-Saxon as a chosen people called to achieve great things fitted well with the radical Puritan idea that human history moved toward the realization of the kingdom of Christ upon earth. "The best of us," wrote William Erbury, a chaplain in Cromwell's model army, "fancy a reign of Christ on earth for a thousand years, and the Saints to reign with him."[18] To many it appeared most appropriate that England above all nations should inaugurate the new godly kingdom. "The elect are no where else but here in England," wrote one commentator, "and so tyed to this place, that if the faith of God's elect were destroyed here, there should be none fav'd . . . England is the place, therefore here and no where else is this faith found."[19] It was commonplace in Puritan thought to see a clear parallel between England's past and the biblical accounts of the history of Israel. England was a new Israel after a long period of betrayals and wanderings finally returning to its convenant with God. John Foxe's *Book of Martyrs* provided a handbook for a proper reading of God's ways with the English nation. God in the past had sent judgment on the English nation, but now was its time of deliverance in which it was to be elevated above all nations. "Now God hath brought England into the *schoole of mercy*," the preacher Edmund Calamy told the Long Parliament in 1642, "and hath placed it *in the highest forme*, and hath made it Captaine of the schoole."[20] Though many of the "saints" were later to be hanged, drawn and quartered for pushing the principles of the revolution to their logical conclusion (some for example refusing to accept as divine revelation the supremacy of parliament as against the rights of man), their vision of a godly kingdom of the elect called to imperial rule continued as an important ingredient in all later expressions of Anglo-Saxonism.

The most forthright pro-Saxon panegyric that appeared in Commonwealth England was Richard Hawkins's *A Discourse of the Nationall Excellencies of England* (1658). It frankly combined patriotic and religious fervor with marked imperialistic sentiments. "And what better time could have been taken," Hawkins commented in his Preface, "to set out the Praises of our Nation then this active Age, which hath inspired men with more sprightly thoughts, introduced the nobler genius of War, warmed the very blood of Age it self, and is likely to be made famous by the exploits of our Nation, which having again got footing on the other side of the Water, may like that little cloud in Ahab's time, which arose Out of the Sea, overspread the Heavens, and once more largely, stretch out its bounds on the very Continent." The English nation from its beginning combined purity of race, martial valor and extraordinary chastity: "The English descend from the people of *Germany* which were called *Saxons*. These by good Authors were esteemed the strongest and valiantest of its Nations, and are reported to have inlarged their bounds further than any other particular Nation did in *Germany*, and carried the terror of their Arms into all parts that lay about them; but especially to have lorded it on the Seas. In a word, they were dreaded for their Arms, and commended for their extraordinary Chastity: so that the English derive from a most noble and pure Fountain, being the off-spring of so valiant and so chaste a people."

Hawkins's dedication to nationalism was left in no doubt: "*What Nation (saith Moses to the Israelites) is so great, which hath Statutes and Judgments so righteous as I set before you this day?* The like question may be asked the English, What Nation is there that hath Statutes and Judgements so righteous as you? What people live so happily under their Law? Certainly not the French, nor the Spaniard, nor the Italian, nor any other that I can name. Why may I not then put in that other part of the question in the Text, *What Nation is so great as England?*"[21]

Hawkins's nationalism was of a peculiarly modern kind: "To see his Nation flourish, be glorious and renowned, is the most eligible fortune that a man can either wish or attain." There was no question but that England's prosperity was a sign of God's election: "For my part, I cannot but at the conclusion of this discourse, admire and praise the bounty of the Divine Providence to England. . . . Let us fear and tremble before our God, for all that good, and for all that prosperity which he hath procured for us."[22]

Thus for Hawkins, England after a long sojourn in the wilderness–a period beginning with the Norman conquest and ending with the triumph of Protestantism–had finally come into its Kingdom.

The new ruling class shared Hawkins's enthusiasm for the new redeemed England. Yet they had anxieties about its permanence. Arguments on behalf of the ancient freedoms were also being used by radicals against a current political system dominated by the wealthy bourgeoisie and gentry. If in Saxon days the voice of the people was heard above that of a king, might it not now be heard above that of an elitist parliament? The power of the military under Cromwell suggested just how threatening to middle-class security a union of discontented officers and men of the rank might be. Those who had gained economic and political ascendancy concluded that stability was preferable to further revolution, which could challenge their gain. The new ruling class was willing "to agree to a restoration of the old law to guarantee the new order."[23] Its leading members decided that a compromise should be reached with the exiled son who was eager to take up a crown.

Charles II, hailed even before his return as a second Arthur descended from the ancient British kings,[24] on the face of it seemed an unlikely champion of Anglo-Saxonism. His marked French and Catholic sympathies were accompanied by a hatred of Puritanism (particularly in its Presbyterian form) and a distinct coolness toward the Church of England. Still he wanted a crown and his past experiences prepared him well for compromise. His new Protestant allies, for their part, were prepared to accept his shortcomings in return for his acquiescence in political affairs. The rigid Calvinism of the earlier part of the century that had inspired the opponents to Charles I, had largely given way to a triumphant Arminianism, which preached the virtue of human activity. The Established Church which had existed "only clandestinely" under the Commonwealth was quite prepared to accept a king of known Catholic sympathies as the price of resumption of status.[25]

In the *Declaration of Breda* heralding his return, Charles informed an expectant nation that he would be "advised" by a "free parliament."[26] Yet for a time after his return any talk about ancient Saxon freedoms was out of favor. Works supporting the antiquity and supremacy of the common law were liable to proscription. John Milton, who had argued that kings and magistrates received their power on trust from the people and could be removed on betrayal of trust, was imprisoned for a time and barely escaped the fate of a traitor. On 16 May 1660 Parliament ordered that his *Eikonoklastes* and *Pro Populo Anglicano Defensio* along with John Goodwin's *Obstruction of Justice* should be burned by the common hangman. Englishmen who wanted to retain court favor were compelled to adjust their view of the past accordingly. Thus myths are modified by political necessities.

In the continuing discussion over the origins of parliament, there was a movement back to pre-Cromwellian theories stressing its dependent and consultative nature. Scholars were not slow to rediscover its beginnings "not in the Anglo-Saxon forests but in the grace of the Plantagenets."[27]

The ambivalent attitude of Englishmen to the Norman Conquest became even more accentuated under the Restoration. As the nobility rose to ascendancy and French culture came into favor, more of them proudly asserted their Norman ancestry.[28] The Conquest, at least among court supporters, was no longer viewed as a great fall from grace that demanded redemption if England were to be healed. The Saxon past might even be praised, provided no threat to royal supremacy was implied. The safest course was to portray the king as somehow Saxon in origin, but the principal conservator of the ancient freedoms.

One of the most interesting of Restoration Saxonists was Sir Winston Churchill, father of the first Duke of Marlborough. In a history dedicated to Charles II he extolled the "*English* or *Saxon*" whose origins reached back to the Flood. In Churchill's account their early history as conquerors of the Britons was "irreconcileable to whatever could be call'd civil or sacred," where "fury and ignorance met in conjunction." But Christianity so transformed their rough nature that, "they became so flexible and obedient to the principles of their new Faith, as men that thought they could never expiate their former inhumanities, but by an excess of zeal, they did as immoderately waste themselves in repairing the ruines they had made, raising so many new Structures, that the number as well as the beauty so far exceeded all those of former times, that it might have been said of their Isle as once of Rome, that it seem'd but one great Monastery."[29]

It is evident that in Churchill's mind the true heroes of English history were not the Norman Conquerors but the brave English who resisted them: "worthy to be as they were then made Immortal; bravely strove with Destiny to save their country from Calamity of Foreign Servitude: but finding that they could not do it, as scorning to outlive their Liberties, they fell round the body of their vanquish'd King."[30] The catastrophe of the Norman Conquest was thus due not to the absence of English courage but rather to "partiality of Fortune." Had the English been permitted to enjoy quietly the benefits of their conquest, they would have established a universal empire more lasting than any that had gone before, but Danish and Norman treachery ended the hope. Happily, in the author's view, in his own lifetime England's promise was revived and her rulers were now "absolute Lords of the Seas." The triumphal return of Charles and the acclamation and prayers that greeted him brought to mind his great sire Charlemagne's welcome by Rome. Thus, the first Churchill historian offered Charles a Saxon past and a call to imperial greatness. Three years later Obadiah Walker underlined Charles's Saxon descent by drawing a striking parallel between Alfred, the greatest of the Saxon kings and Charles his "*vera* & *naturali*" heir.[31]

Of all historical writers, John Milton was the least swayed by the prevailing political myths of the day. Of a highly independent mind, he refused to subscribe to the portrait of the early English painted by either Saxon or British enthusiasts.

In his major historical work, *The History of Britain* (1670), Milton cast doubts on all accounts of the history of pre-Roman Britain: "nothing certain, either by tradition, History, or Ancient Fame hath hitherto been left us." To him what appeared oldest, "hath by the greater part of judicious Antiquaries been long rejected for a modern Fable." The Brutus legend "and the entire Trojan pretence" he viewed with tolerant scepticism.[32] He declined to take seriously the popularly accepted account of Britain as the first nation, in the days of King Lucius, to have publicly accepted Christianity, a version accepted by scholars like Holinshed, Stow and Speed. He abandoned an intended epic on the story of Arthur because "his studies had convinced him that there was no more truth in it than there was in the story of Brutus."[33] Still, in his *History* he was not adverse to retelling those "reputed tales," if for no other reason than "in favour of English Poets and Rhetoricians." Milton, the Puritan, did not spare the Britons. Their many miseries and desolations were "brought by divine hand on a perverse Nation."[34]

If Milton was critical of historical accounts derived from Geoffrian sources in praise of British antiquity, he was hardly less so of those presented by Saxon panegyrists. Milton was a defender of "liberty rightly used" and was not confident that the irrational temperament of the early Saxons rendered them apt subjects for freedom. He declined to interpret the Danish or Norman invasions as conquests carried out by aliens against another race. Rather, since most of the Anglo-Saxons allegedly came from Jutland and Anglin, and "the Danes and Normans are the same," then it followed that the Danes simply conquered their own posterity, and "the Normans afterwards, none but antienter Normans." His portrayal of the Anglo-Saxons at the beginning of the ninth century as a people, "as wicked as the Britans were at their arrival, brok'n with luxuries and sloth" was one calculated to please neither Saxon nor Celt. The religious character of Saxon England, which was extolled by his contemporary Winston Churchill, to Milton represented nothing but the triumph of idolatry and sloth and brought forth only "vain and delusive visions."[35] Popular beliefs about England's early conversion to Christianity were treated with complete scepticism. For Milton it was far more to England's honor to have been the first nation (in the person of Wyclif) to have "set up as standard for the recovery of lost truth and blow the first Evangelick Trumpet to the Nations."[36] On parliament's role as an ancient protector of freedom, he was equally incredulous: it was "a Norman or French word, a monument of our ancient servitude."[37]

It was Milton's deep-rooted antinomianism which pushed him to take a far more critical approach to accepted opinions than most of his contemporaries. As the Glorious Revolution approached, the Whig opponents to the Catholic James found that a careful selection from his writings could be helpful to their cause. By the beginning of the eighteenth century, with Anglo-Saxonism once more on the rise, Milton's reservations about Gothicism were forgotten and he was posthumously enlisted as a faithful Saxonist and Whig precursor.[38]

The waning of Anglo-Saxonism as a dominant social myth during the Restoration was more apparent than real. Though the myth was tempered somewhat in the face of political necessities, solid work continued to be done by scholars in deepening an understanding of the language and customs of Saxon times. Increasingly men associated with Cambridge and Oxford assumed responsibility for this work.

One of the greatest needs for an improved study of the language was met with the publication of William Somner's Anglo-Saxon dictionary. Two years earlier Somner had received the stipend of the Cambridge Lectureship in Anglo-Saxon and this enabled him to complete a work which provided a much needed tool for students and initiated a new period of growth in Anglo-Saxon scholarship. Somner undertook his work at the urging of Meric Casaubon who himself had produced a study, *De Quatuor Linquis* (1650), praising the virtues of the Saxon language. Another Cambridge scholar, Robert Sheringham, combined a keen interest in Saxon origins with a complete trust in Geoffrey's *History of the British Kings*. While a royalist exile in Holland during the Civil War, he had developed an interest in Teutonic mythology. On his return he pursued studies on the various races that inhabited the British Isles. In his major work, *De Anglorum Gentis Origine* (1670), a mixture of legend and fact, he had the highest praise for the superior qualities of the Saxons. A more distinguished scholar, Thomas Gale, fellow of Trinity, edited important chronicles, including the texts of Gildas and Nennius and Eddi's *Life of Wilfrid.*

Oxford could claim its own share of Saxon scholars and gradually eclipsed Cambridge. Francis Junius was perhaps the principal inspirer of Saxon studies at Oxford. Junius was born in Heidelberg and came to England in 1621 as tutor to the son of Thomas Howard, Earl of Arundel. He had early developed an interest in Teutonic dialects and comparative philology. In England he maintained a close association with Oxford, and through his special friendship with Thomas Marshall of Lincoln College, himself an ardent Saxonist, he helped create a continuing interest in early English studies. In time Oxford would absorb "every branch of Old English learning—theological, historical, antiquarian and linguistic."[39]

The continuing labor of scholars in exploring and commenting on the English past was of critical importance in maintaining Anglo-Saxonism as a national myth which fired the imagination of a people with expanding imperial pretensions. In an age increasingly influenced by scientific modes of thought, some form of rational validation of historic myths was necessary, if such myths were to serve their purpose. The fate of Geoffrey of Monmouth's account of origins amply demonstrated that a national myth of scant historical basis could not survive in a rationalistic age. Anglo-Saxonism could not have thrived throughout the seventeenth century and served so well as parliament's good servant had not its creators consciously sought to ground it in historical reality.

Coincidental with a growing pride of race among native Englishmen was the parallel development of the slave trade and the accompanying victimization of black people. Though explicit racist arguments assigning the Negro to a lower order of humanity would not be heard until the last half of the eighteenth century, it is clear that in the seventeenth century Englishmen regarded the black slave as a plaything or chattel as much at the disposal of his master as any other bit of property. This attitude to the Negro—which explains so much about the general readiness to exploit him for personal gain—had roots reaching back to classical civilization and was subsequently reinforced by Christianity, but the growing pride of race that was becoming a marked feature of English nationalism did nothing to promote a more sympathetic understanding of a black people so obviously non-Germanic in origin and it enabled a growing number of English merchants and entrepreneurs (fully supported by king, parliament and the entire legal confraternity) to participate in good conscience in a highly lucrative enterprise.

Chapter IV

A MYTH CONFIRMED

The developments of 1688-89 which brought William, Prince of Orange, to the throne of England have had a unique importance in confirming for generations to come the attitude of Englishmen to their cultural origins. The "muddled incoherent events . . . that had nearly spelt anarchy and ruin to the English nation"[1] were in time idealized and interpreted as a spontaneous national rising in defense of established religious and political freedoms threatened by the absolutism of a Catholic king. Though in fact the greater part of the nation stood aside "while the vital decisions were taken, almost at random, by a few noblemen and their friends,"[2] belief in the heroic nature of what came to be called the Glorious Revolution grew into an essential ingredient of the national mythology.

The perplexity of the first Whig supporters of the new foreign king is illustrated by the attempted revision of the hitherto negative view of William the Conqueror. An effort was made to cast him as an archetype of William III, a predestined deliverer from across the seas with a mission to restore ancient Saxon liberties.

The most extravagant statement of this view appeared in Sir William Temple's *An Introduction to the History of England* (1695). Temple, a long-time admirer of the Prince of Orange, portrayed the first William as an intrepid conqueror of excelling virtue, wisdom and valor, whose first care was, "for the due administration and execution of Laws and Justice throughout his Realm." In Temple's interpretation it was the Conqueror's resolve, "to govern the Kingdom as a legal Prince, and leave the ancient Laws and Liberties of the *English* Nation as they had before enjoyed them."[3] Though he noted deviations from William's high purpose, Temple judged, that on balance, England gained much from the Conquest, viz., extension of possessions abroad; increased naval power; refinement of language, customs, and manners; and increased international prestige. The parallels with the reign of the new William were clearly there to be drawn by any enterprising Whig.

Temple was at pains to emphasize that the liberties maintained by William I were an inheritance from Gothic ancestors of outstanding virtue, a people divinely elected to exercise dominion: "For, of all the Northern nations, the Goths were esteemed the most civil, orderly and virtuous; and are for such commended by Saint Augustine and Salvian, who make their conquests to have been given them by the justice of God, as a reward of their virtue, and a punishment upon the Roman provinces for the viciousness and corruption of their lives and government."[4]

Temple's Gothic enthusiasm was matched by John Toland, the celebrated deist and editor of Milton. He argued vigorously in support of the rejection of James and applauded the Act of Succession in its limiting of the monarchy to Protestants. In his *Anglia Libera* (1701) he insisted that it was a part of the traditional English constitution to reserve to the people the right of exclusion. In Saxon times succession was so regulated, "that you always hear almost of every King's *Election* before his Coronation." That this tradition lived on there was no doubt in Toland's mind. For the benefit of his readers he would: "deduce this Argument from William the Norman to this very time; first to undeceive those (or their adherents) who may think themselves injur'd for being now set aside, tho they be next of kin; and secondly to show those appointed in the present Limitation of the Crown, that they have no other Right or Claim than the good Opinion and free Choice of the People of England." Toland's view of what happened in 1688-89 was unambiguous: James II, ardent papist and puppet of France "made such havock of all Laws human and divine . . . that at last the whole Nation rose up in arms against him, and call'd in the Prince of Orange to their assistance, whereupon he abdicated the government."[5]

There was a distinctly utilitarian bent to Toland's concept of freedom which well suited an aggressive age dedicated to the pursuit of gain. This attitude is strikingly demonstrated in the following passage: "The preminence of a free State does consist in the injoyment of every thing which contributes to perfect the Felicity of mankind. The inhabitants of this Country are numerous, industrious, sober, wealthy, and martial; Liberty and Laws secure 'em in their possessions, which makes 'em as vigilant and valiant in Defense of the Government as to preserve their own Lives; the buildings are constantly in repair, excelling in Magnificence and Architecture; the Lands are improved with all manners of culture, for Ornament and Delight, as well as the Profit of the Owners; the public Roads, Walks, Bridges, Edifices, and the like are equally stately and commodious, the Rivers and Harbors are full of Ships which import whatever is useful or pretious in any Part of the Universe, and export the Superfluity of native Productions to such as need 'em elsewhere."[6]

Toland, taking his lead from John Locke, the philosopher of the new age, while readily subscribing to the doctrine of sovereignty of the people, would have limited political rights in practice to men of property. As Daniel Defoe caustically put it, "There can be no pretence of government till they that have the property consent."[7]

Toland's pragmatism marks a shift in the pre-occupations of those that controlled the destiny of England: as they felt more institutionally secure, passions that were formerly spent in religious and political controversies were now turned more to the practical business of creating profitable commercial enterprises. Anglo-Saxonism was adapted accordingly. As well as standing for an inherited Gothic genius for creating and maintaining free institutions it came also to champion good business sense and the virtue of prosperity.

There were some, however, who were reluctant to subscribe to the prevailing theme of a valorous and virtuous Saxon ancestry as the font of present English achievements, a refrain repeated a thousand times since first formulated by Camden and Verstegen. Daniel Defoe, in particular, subjected it to savage if rough satire. In *The True-born Englishman* (1701) he heaped scorn on the idea of the English as a unified race of superior origin; rather they were a mongrel people made up of the dregs of Europe:

> The Romans first with Julius Caesar came,
> Including all the Nations of that Name,
> Gauls, Greeks, and Lombards; and by Computation,

Auxiliaries or slaves of ev'ry Nation.
With Hengist, Saxons; Danes with Sueno came,
In search of Plunder, not in search of Fame.
Scots, Picts, and Irish from the Hiberian shore:
And Conquering William brought the Normans O're

All these their Barb'rous offspring left behind,
The dregs of Armies, they of all Mankind;
Blended with Britains, who before were here,
Of whom the Welch ha' blest the Character.
From this Amphibious Ill-born Mob began
That vain ill-natured thing, an Englishman.[8]

Defoe scoffed at the claim to Saxon origin made by so many upperclass Englishmen:

Of sixty thousand English gentlemen,
Whose Names and Arms in Registers remain,
We challenge all our Heralds to declare
Ten Families which English-Saxon are.[9]

In his satire, *Jure Divino,* he characterized the Saxon kingdoms (as indeed all kingdoms) as being built, not on freedom, but "on Violence and Blood." The right to property, so cherished by the middle class, took its origin not from any natural right (contra Locke), but from violence:

Our Ancestors obtain'd the Kingdom thus,
And left the ill-got Recompence to us:
The very Lands we all along enjoy'd,
They ravish'd from the People they destroy'd.

Thus to claim distinction because of any alleged pre-Norman ancestry was to Defoe absurd. "We are very fond of some Families," he commented "because they can be trac'd beyond the Conquest, whereas, indeed, the farther back the worse, as being the nearer ally'd to a Race of Robbers and Thieves."[10]

The common-sense approach of Defoe to the question of racial superiority was echoed to a degree by Jonathan Swift. Contrary to the view that the people of England were of a genius and temper which made them peculiarly apt subjects for freedom, he asserted: "I think it is a great Error to count upon the Genius of a Nation as a standing argument in all Ages; since there is hardly a spot of ground in Europe, where the Inhabitants have not frequently and entirely changed their Temper and Genius. Neither can I see any Reason why the Genius of a Nation should be more fixed in the point of government, than in their Morals, their Learning, their Religion, their common Humour and Conversation, their Diet, and their Complexion; which do all notoriously vary almost in every Age, and may every one of them have great Effects upon Mens notions of government." Swift maintained that there was a natural balance of power in free states which proceeded from the use of reason by the legislators far more than from any Gothic racial tradition.[11] He, nevertheless, accepted parliament as a peculiarly Gothic institution, implanted "by the Saxon princes, who first introduced them into this island, from the same original with the other Gothic forms of government in most parts of Europe."[12]

In questioning extravagant statements on racial origin, men like Defoe and, to a lesser degree, Swift were the exception. More in harmony with the mood of the day was the Gothicism of the Whig, Edmund Gibson, Bishop of Lincoln and later of London. The dedication to George I of his translation of Camden's *Britannia* glows with pride in the common Saxon origin which linked the Hanoverian king with his English subjects: "It is this alliance which has made us happy in your Majesty and your Royal Family, and which intitles You to the love of every subject, as a Prince of our own blood; especially, when that indearment of blood is inforced by so much graciousness of temper and disposition. But the ensuing work points out a relation between your Majesty and these kingdoms, of a far more ancient date. Not only our histories, but our language, our laws, our customs, our names of persons and names of places, do all abundantly testify, that the greatest part of your Majesty's subjects, are of Saxon original. And, if we inquire from whence our Saxon ancestors came, we shall find, that it was from your Majesty's dominions in Germany, where their brethren, who staid behind, spread themselves through a noble and spacious country, which still retains their name; so that the main body of your people, in both nations, are really descended from one and the same common stock; and now, after a disunion of so many ages, they live again under this protection and influence of the same common Parent." Gibson believed that Englishmen were doubly blessed in their German king, for not only did he unite two people of common origin, but also stood as a staunch defender of Protestantism, "in the protection whereof against the tyrannies of Popery, your Majesty has exerted your power and interest in a most distinguishing manner; for which you have the prayers of the present age, and your memory will be blessed to all posterity."[13]

The Whiggism of Gibson was paralleled in the writings of the historian and pamphleteer, John Oldmixon. He maintained that the present constitution was a great gift inherited from Gothic ancestors and that Englishmen had protected its legacy better than all other nations. In spite of efforts by political and religious "flatterers" throughout the reigns of the four Stuart monarchs to destroy the ancient constitution, through the Glorious Revolution it was secured for posterity. Of the Saxon origin of parliament Oldmixon had not the slightest doubt. On the authority of Henry Spelman he triumphantly asserted, "The Witenagemot was the same thing among the Saxons, as the Parliament is now-a-days with us."[14] (He completely ignored the work of the Restoration historian Robert Brady, who, also drawing on the research of Spelman, argued with great cogency that William I by establishing feudal tenures had radically altered the English constitutional system, and that parliament in its origins could only be a type of feudal council directly linked to the tenure of the crown.)[15] Oldmixon's Gothicism was very close to that of his contemporary, John Molesworth, who distinguished between the *nominal* Whigs, "who are worse than any sort of men," and the *real* Whig, "who is exactly for keeping up to the strictness of the old Gothick Constitution."[16]

One of the strongest defenses of the immemorial origins of the Englishman's "spirit of liberty" came somewhat unexpectedly from the pen of the Tory, Henry St. John, Viscount Bolingbroke. He skilfully used what can only be called a Whig interpretation of history to attack the policy of Sir Robert Walpole. Weekly throughout 1730-31, Bolingbroke published, under the pseudonym Humphrey Oldcastle, his *Remarks on the History of England* in his journal, *The Craftsman*. Walpole countered by reprinting Robert Brady's *History* in his weekly, *The London Journal*.[17]

Bolingbroke rhapsodized on the long and unbroken dedication to liberty that characterized the history of the English nation. Englishmen could take pride that, "the Romans, those Masters of the World, maintain'd their Liberty little more than seven centuries; and that Britain, which was a free Nation above seventeen hundred years ago, is so at this Hour." First there were the Britons, who as a people of spirit and sense, "knew the Ends of Government, and obliged their Governors to pursue those Ends." Then came the Saxons, who while "submitting to the Yoke of Rome in matters of Religion," nevertheless "were far from giving up the Freedom of their Gothick Institutions of Government." Though the Saxons, following the ancient Germanic custom, initially selected their leaders only to direct them in time of war, in time, the latter assumed the trappings of kings. But significantly, "the supreme Power center'd in the *Micklemote* or *Wittagenmote*, composed of the King, the Lords, and the Saxon Freemen, that original sketch of a British Parliament." "The Principles of the Saxon Commonwealth," Bolingbroke went on to observe, "were therefore very democratical; and these Principles prevail'd through all subsequent Changes."[18]

Bolingbroke neatly made even William the Conqueror an unwitting conservator of Saxon freedoms. While the Norman king and his two sons on many occasions ruled as absolute rather than limited monarchs, yet "neither he, nor they could destroy the old Constitution, because neither he, nor they, could extinguish the old Spirit of Liberty." Indeed the contrary was the case: "The

Normans and other Strangers, who settled here, were soon seized with it themselves, instead of inspiring a Spirit of Slavery into the Saxons."[19]

As Bolingbroke was presenting his eulogy on ancient English liberties in the *Craftsman*, Voltaire was completing his *Letters Concerning the English Nation*, the fruit of an extended visit to England. Voltaire, out of favor in France, had come to England in May, 1726, and remained until 1729. He had met Bolingbroke on several previous occasions during the latter's exile in France (1714-25) and developed a deep admiration for him and for things English. His two and a half years' visit confirmed his affection for English institutions. However, he scoffed at the suggestion that liberty as experienced in England was an ancient Gothic inheritance; rather, it "sprung from the quarrels of Tyrants." He rejected scornfully the commonly held opinion that the ancient Germanic peoples enjoyed free institutions which they brought to other parts of Europe: "The Barbarians who came from the shores of the Baltick, and settled in the rest of Europe, brought with them the form of government call'd States or Parliaments, about which so much noise is made, and which are so little understood. Kings indeed were not absolute in those days, but then the people were more wretched upon that very account, and more completely enslav'd. The Chiefs of these savages who laid waste France, Italy, Spain and England, made themselves Monarchs. Their generals divided among themselves the several countries they had conquer'd, whence sprung those Margraves, those Peers, those Barons, those petty tyrants, who often contested with their Sovereigns for the spoils of whole nations. These were birds of prey, with an Eagle for Doves, whose blood the Victorious was to suck. Every nation, instead of being govern'd by one Master, was trampled upon by an hundred Tyrants." Voltaire was no less severe on those who venerated Magna Charta as a testimony to the Englishman's love of liberty: "This Great Charter which is consider'd as the sacred origin of the English Liberties, shews in it self how little Liberty was known."[20]

Whatever one may think of Voltaire's cynical historical judgments he, far more than most of his contemporaries, avoided the fallacy of anachronism; a reading of the past as a mirror of the present became the hallmark of the Whig historian for generations to come. Voltaire was to be no less scornful of French historians who, following the lead of Count Boulainvilliers, argued fiercely for the Germanic origin of the French aristocracy: "There is not a single great family in France," he wrote, "which can produce, I will not say the least proof, but the least presumption of being descended from a Frankish founder."[21]

Another great Frenchman who lived in England around the same period—from the Autumn of 1729 to the Spring of 1731—and commented on her institutions was Baron de Montesquieu. He was destined to have an immense influence in spreading the idea of the inherent superiority of the English political system over all other forms, a superiority rooted in its Germanic origin. His observations on England were written in 1734 and were eventually published in 1748 as Book XI of his influential *De L'Esprit des Lois*. Montesquieu held up England as an example to be emulated by all nations interested in establishing a sound political system. England was the only country in the world that had "for the direct end of its constitution political liberty." It was clear to Montesquieu, following Tacitus, that it was in the forests of Germany "that this beautiful system was invented."[22] Montesquieu's book, one of the most influential political tracts ever written, was widely read in England and America and added powerful support to the advocates of Anglo-Saxonism.

By mid-century belief in the inherited genius of an English people essentially Germanic in origin had become so pervasive that it was seldom if ever seriously questioned. Men of the Enlightenment who prided themselves on their ability to discern the spurious and implausible seemed to set aside their scepticism where racial origin was concerned. No one illustrates this better than David Hume, the prince of sceptics. He had the highest praise for the manners and political institutions of the ancient Germans and especially in their Saxon branch. The Germans carried "to the highest pitch the virtue of valour and love of liberty." Their government, established on the ruins of a despotic Rome, "was always extremely free" and "still preserve[s] an air of independence and legal administration which distinguish European nations from all others." The debt European civilization owed to the Germans was incalculable, for if it "maintains" sentiments of liberty, honour, equity, and valour, superior to the rest of mankind, it owes these advantages chiefly to the seeds implanted by those generous barbarians." Hume portrayed the Saxons as continuing in England the liberty they enjoyed in their country of origin. He accepted without question the authority of Tacitus: "the picture of a fierce and bold liberty, which is drawn by the masterly pencil of Tacitus will suit those founders of the English government."[23]

Hume's account of a despotic Rome in decay giving way to a manly freedom-loving Germanic people who in time revivified Europe will be drawn out and completed by the greatest historian of the age, Edward Gibbon. In a famous passage in his *Decline and Fall* (1776) Gibbon contrasts the decadence of the Romans with the vigor of the Germanic invaders: "This diminutive stature of mankind . . . was daily sinking below the old standard, and the Roman world was indeed peopled by a race of pygmies, when the fierce giants of the north broke in and mended the puny breed."[24] The enormous popularity of Hume and Gibbon assured that few literate Englishmen were left unaware of their proud heritage.

Even a radical republican writer like Catherine Macaulay could not resist the spell of the rampant Anglo-Saxonism of her day. In her *History of England* (1763) she traced English rights to Saxon origins, rights purchased "by the toil and blood of the most exalted individuals that ever adorned humanity." Though she lamented the poisoning of the constitution by political corruption, she defended parliament as a precious institution of Gothic origin which carried within itself "many latent resources to preserve liberty."[25] She maintained that those who had brought Charles I to heel were in reality reaching back to reestablish ancient freedoms once held by every Englishman. The Petition of Rights, for example, "though it did not produce a change in the constitution, yet it confirmed to the subject every privilege which their ancestors had, for any length of time, enjoyed since the Norman Conquest had given the fatal blow to that enlarged system of liberty introduced by the Saxons." The Civil War itself was a reaction against "the numberless instances in which Charles had violated the law of the land," violations which "roused the attention of the nation to develop the real genius of the constitution." It was Macaulay's conviction that the English people made a tragic error when they restored hereditary right instead of "recurring to the more wholesome principles of the Saxon constitution."[26]

Perhaps in no document of the century was the case for Gothic superiority put more confidently than in the popular and oft-cited anonymous work, *An Historical Essay on the English Constitution* (1771). The mode of government introduced by the Saxons was presented as perfection of its kind: "I am of the opinion that if ever God almighty did concern himself about forming a government for mankind to live happily under, it was that which was established in England, by our Saxon forefathers." In its Germanic original it was "as far superior to the Greek and Roman commonwealth, as these surpassed the government of the Medes, and Persians." No other system of government protected the natural rights of man as well: "Every man, under that institution, was preserved in his natural, and equal rights whether he were rich or poor." Though the English constitution was "much impaired, maimed, and disfigured, it hath stood the admiration of many ages; and still remains the most noble, and ancient monument of Gothick antiquity."[27]

The author's interpretation of the Norman Conquest was entirely predictable. The Normans temporarily destroyed the elective character of parliament, but it was restored to its rightful position of authority by the immortal barons responsible for the Magna Charta and more recently by those who had opposed Charles I. The principle was clear: "whatever is of Saxon establishment is truly constitutional, but whatever is Norman is heterogeneous to it, and partakes of a tyrannical spirit."

In King Alfred, the Saxons possessed "a prince of the most exalted merit, that ever graced the English throne." He captured in his own person the full genius of his people: "He was a great warriour, an able statesman, and a person of great learning, he knew and loved the constitution of his country; and above all, was an honest man, and the common friend of mankind. It was a singular providence to this kingdom, that the new modelling of the government, should fall under the management of so great a genius."[28]

Thus the author of what was intended as a radical tract in defense of annual parliament offered to English readers an idealized interpretation of their past that was on the way to becoming a part of the folk wisdom of the day. The image of a full-fledged pre-Norman parliamentary democracy with a recognition of human rights that would have been the envy of any eighteenth-century political radical had an understandable appeal. Even writers who made a conscious effort to interpret the past in terms of its own standards and interests were beguiled by it.

Thus Robert Robinson in his *Political Cathechism* (1784) could shrewdly observe: "our constitution, like our language, is a fineness produced by the friction of contending interests," but he gave it to be understood, to quote Professor Butterfield, "that the declaration of rights and the British constitution go back to the time of Alfred."[29] Ten years earlier Thomas Jefferson argued for American independence on the grounds that just as much as their Saxon ancestors, who had established in Britain "that system of laws which had so long been the glory and protection of that Country," American colonists had a natural right to construct a free society in America.[30]

The group that could claim no link with Saxon forebearers and continued to suffer the greatest political and legal disabilities was of course the black population of the British Colonies. Though by the 1780s the slavery abolition movement, led by men like Granville Sharp and William Wilberforce, was beginning to have some slight impact, it met with the stoutest opposition from plantation owners, merchants, naval men, and their parliamentary supporters, who found it inconceivable that freedoms derived from Saxon ancestors could be extended to black men. The attitude of Edward Long, author of the well received *The History of Jamaica* (1774), was typical. Long had served as judge of the Vice-Admiralty Court in Jamaica and accordingly spoke with authority. He argued persuasively that it was repugnant to the human mind that "British freedoms" should be extended to a colored people so obviously void of all genius and "almost incapable of making any progress in civility or science." Rather than encouraging in black men "a high, a liberal, and independent spirit," Long thought it best that they be taught "to consider implicit submission to superiors as the greatest of all virtues, and a boundless, blind obedience of authority, as the essence of all civil duties."[31] Long, as much a dedicated Saxonist as Hume and Jefferson, questioned the black man's full humanity.

Of all publicists for the inherited excellence of the English political system, none was more eloquent than Edmund Burke, a supporter of the continuance of slavery, but reformed and regulated.[32] A writer of the highest distinction, he did more than any other man of his age to fix in the mind of his own and later generations belief in the providential nature of the British constitution as it developed through the ages and was finally confirmed by the Glorious Revolution. Burke was the theoretician of the Whig faction led by the Marquess of Rockingham, the successor to Robert Walpole and the Pelhams, who found themselves out of office when George III came to the throne in 1760. The Rockinghamites, resentful of their loss of power, presented themselves as the preservers of the authentic English political tradition, while painting their opponents as men set on subverting the constitution.

In the Burkean vision the British constitution was seen as a reflection of a divine law which progressively revealed itself through the historical evolution of civilized states. Of a Platonic cast of mind, Burke was somehow able to see the archaic oligarchical system of his own day, one dominated by a clique of wealthy landholders and merchants, as representing the essence of political wisdom, a sacred patrimony with beginnings in the mists of history and passed down from generation to generation to his own day. "We wished at the period of the [Glorious] Revolution, and do now wish," wrote Burke, "to derive all we posses as *an inheritance from our fore-fathers*."[33] In Burke's mind it was foolhardy for men to seek to construct their institutions on any *a priori* rational model; rather, their salvation, both religiously and politically, lay in a participation in an historic process which ultimately was rooted in the Divine mind. The doctrine of immemorial origins, which so appealed to the seventeenth-century Cokeans, received its loftiest expression in Burke's writings. His literary magic cast its spell on unwary readers for generations to come and served to obscure the deep conservatism and class prejudice that underlay his thought. Though he avoided a form of Gothicism which narrowly identified the Anglo-Saxons as uniquely God's chosen people, his elitist philosophy, which interpreted the present order of things as of God's election, did much to maintain a climate of opinion wherein essentially racist arguments were sympathetically heard. Though the Burkean image of English society became less and less realistic as England industrialized and underwent reform, it persisted in the form of a political myth which influenced almost every major nineteenth-century historical commentator.

As England successfully weathered the unsettling storms of the American and French revolutions and her leaders gave more of their energies to the expansion and exploitation of a vast colonial empire, confidence in the predestined greatness of the Anglo-Saxon people grew apace. Even the events associated with the rapid expansion of America were interpreted as further proof of the enterprising virtue and special calling of England's exported Protestant sons. Thus a century that had begun with so much uncertainty ended with England on the verge of becoming the world's greatest imperial power. Everywhere there seemed evidence that the new century would witness unparalleled achievements and the full flowering of Anglo-Saxon genius. A host of panegyrists were at hand eager to proclaim the triumph.

Chapter V

A MYTH TRIUMPHANT

Progress and Historiography

The nineteenth century was England's century. No country emerged from the troubled French revolutionary era with leaders possessing such confidence in the basic soundness of their political and economic institutions and with higher expectations for the future. The social unrest flowing from rapid industrialization, while causing anxiety to the ruling class, did little to shake the basic confidence of those convinced of England's destiny.

From the sixteenth century onwards a conviction had gradually formed in the Englishman's mind that he was peculiarly manly, honorable, apt for leadership and that his social institutions, of ancient Saxon pedigree, were superior to those of any other people. Looking to the future, he felt nothing was impossible. "Above all things, men and women believe me," proclaimed William Gladstone at the height of Victorian opulence, "the world grows better from century to century, because God reigns supreme, from generation to generation. Let pessimism be absent from our minds, and let optimism throw its glory over all our souls and all our lives henceforth and forever."[1] The new-found faith in progress merits examination within a broader context.

If one could isolate a single idea to represent the *Zeitgeist* of the nineteenth century it undoubtedly would be that of constant human progress. As a directive force moving Western society to an ever higher form of civilization, the notion of progress was accepted as axiomatic by most major thinkers. Conceived by men of the Enlightenment as a secular substitute for the ancient belief in divine providential rule, it dominated European thought by the end of the French Revolution. In association with neo-nationalism and industrialism, it provided the dynamism which led to Western world hegemony.

It was the great German philosopher, Immanuel Kant, who provided a philosophical and moral framework in which the new theory of progress could be viewed. In his *Conjectural Beginning of Human History* and *Idea for a Universal History* he gave coherent expression to a philosophy of history which located the meaning and end of history within the historical process itself.

Kant believed he saw in history a movement toward the realization of good, what he called "the progression of freedom." History moved at a level transcending the intention and conscious direction of men and its movement always served a moral function. The process was a unitary one proceeding inexorably to a predetermined end. The helplessness of men confronted with the necessity of history was only apparent and did not negate the possibility of human freedom, for the world was so ordered that morality and freedom were mutually reinforcing.

Following the lead of Kant, later thinkers worked out theories of an absolute historicism in which the historical explanation became an all-embracing and sufficient explanation of temporal activity. History was seen as a justification of whatever is, a theory that in time was bound to be well received by statesmen and industrialists set on imperial expansion and domination. Hegel led the way in identifying the progress of universal history with Germanic political thought and culture. He asserted that the final stage of history was reached with the development of Christian Europe and specifically with the full manifestation in his own time of the Germanic Spirit—"The German Spirit is the Spirit of the new World."[2]

While German political philosophers and historians wove their mystical theories about national greatness in isolation from the social realities that prevailed in the economically and politically backward German states, their English brothers participated actively in the shaping of a society busily engaged in creating a world empire. While one might justly anticipate that the rational concept of natural rights—particularly the individual's right to property—would have greater appeal for Englishmen than any form of German idealism, still, there was a strain in the latter that held a peculiar attraction for them. The theme of the unique genius and destiny of the Germanic people was one with which they were long familiar and with which they could readily identify. Baron Henry Lytton Bulwer, an advanced liberal spokesman, echoed a common refrain when, in a stirring parliamentary speech in 1832, he linked English political and religious freedom with the liberty of ancient Germany: "With that land, and the people of that land, the people of this country must be ever connected. It was in the free forests of Germany that the infant genius of our liberty was nursed. It was from the free altars of Germany that the light of our purer religion first arose."[3]

The related theme of progress was eagerly embraced by most English leaders. A lone exception was John Henry Newman, who lamented in 1832: "The country seems to me to be in a dream, being drugged with this fallacious notion of its superiority to other countries and times."[4] Lord Macaulay's proud boast that the history of England "is emphatically the history of progress" and that the English race "have become the greatest and most highly civilized people that ever the world saw"[5] was to be repeated in varied forms by a multitude of enthusiasts throughout the remainder of the century.

Inevitably for more and more Englishmen race became the principal determinant of personal character and social progress. As the highly popular and eccentric anatomist, Robert Knox, M.D., stated it in 1850: "With me, race or heredity descent is everything; it stamps the man."[6] Writing in 1866, Luke Owen Pike, a harsh critic of the prevailing Teutomania, observed: "There are probably few educated Englishmen living who have not in their infancy been taught that the English nation is a nation of almost pure Teutonic blood, that its political constitution, its social customs, its internal prosperity, the success of its arms, and the number of its colonies have all followed necessarily upon the arrival, in three vessels, of certain German warriors under the command of Hengist and Horsa."[7]

The climax of the crescendo of praise for the Anglo-Saxon inheritance will be reached at the turn of the century with Rudyard Kipling's patriotic eulogies to the English race: "Truly," he told an appreciative English audience, "ye come of The Blood."[8]

Of all professions none served the cause of progress and Anglo-Saxonism more faithfully than historians. Gifted commentators such as Lord Macaulay, Thomas Carlyle, John Kemble, Goldwin Smith, John R. Green, William Stubbs, James Anthony Froude,

Charles Kingsley, Edward Freeman, Lord Acton, dilated upon the greatness of the English race and its proud heritage. All were confident that their accounts were somehow more objective than any that had come before, for history, it was believed, had finally come of age as a critical science.

At the beginning of the century a renewed interest in the ancient past was sparked by Sharon Turner's *History of the Anglo-Saxons* (1799-1805). His work, based on painstaking and comprehensive research, provided a wealth of new information on Anglo-Saxon literature and history. It appeared at a time when the Romantic movement was directing men's minds toward the past and was enthusiastically received. Though Turner had no sympathy for the new school of historical criticism developing in Germany—it appeared to challenge too many traditional religious beliefs—his work was filled with Whig conceptions. A casual reader might easily assume that the period between the days of Alfred and the Hanoverians was but a brief interlude during which the original seed of Saxon genius germinated, ridded itself of impurities and blossomed to full maturity. Turner simply assumed that the English of his own day were one with the ancient Saxons.

Turner did not conceal the rudeness and brutality of the early Germanic tribes, but he presented as their saving grace a love of individual independence and a high sense of political liberty. These characteristics were to become, "the source of our greatest improvements in legislature, society, knowledge, and general comfort." Turner portrayed the nomadic mind as a peculiarly apt instrument for the creation of free social institutions: "The Nomadic mind is a mind of great energy and sagacity, in the pursuits and necessities peculiar to that state; and has devised many principles of laws, governments, customs, and institutions, which have been superior to others that the earlier civilized have established.

"The Saxons, Franks, Burgundians, Goths and Northmen have been distinguished by these characteristics."[9]

Turner developed the theme that among Germanic tribes the

Saxons were recognized by their contemporaries as "superior to others in energy, strength, and warlike fortitude." In addition, nature had provided them, "with the germ of those amiable qualities which have become the national character of their descendants. . . ." It was from such sterling ancestors that "a nation has, in the course of twelve centuries, been formed, which, inferior to none in every moral and intellectual merit, is superior to every other in the love and possession of useful liberty: a nation which cultivates with equal success the elegancies of art, the ingenious labours of industry, the energies of war, the researches of science, and the richest production of genius." In Turner's judgment, of all the contributions bequeathed to the English none was more noteworthy than the institution of parliament: "If we had no other evidence of the political wisdom of our Gothic or Teutonic ancestors than their institution of the witena-gemots, or national parliaments, this happy and wise invention would be sufficient to entitle them to our veneration and gratitude." Of the witenagemot's identity with the modern English parliament Turner had few doubts: "After many years' consideration of the question, I am inclined to believe, that the Anglo-Saxon witenagemot very much resembled our present parliament, in the orders and persons that composed it; and that the members, who attended as representatives, were chosen by classes and analogous to those who now possess the elective franchise."[10]

Turner believed that the rudimentary beginnings of the Anglican Church were clearly visible in Saxon times. The form of hierarchy was episcopal; the people were strongly exhorted to study the scripture and thus "the Anglo-Saxon church formed a remarkable contrast to the Roman Catholic hierarchy of subsequent ages." Doctrines on the Eucharist were free from later Roman corruptions: "It was certain that transubstantiation was not the established or universal belief of the Anglo-Saxons." It was true that monasticism flourished, but "when monasteries were founded among the Anglo-Saxons, mankind had not attained or noticed the experience of all their effects, and the visible good which they achieved prevented their evils from being felt." But the law of progress assured that inimical things would be discarded and thus the growth of the infant Anglo-Saxon Church proceeded along wholesome lines: "New agencies occurred afterwards to rear this infant to a noble youth. Better views of religion have since united with expanded science and progressive reason to conduct the national character and mind to a still superior manhood. Each preceding stage was necessary to the formation of the subsequent. Each has produced its appropriate utilities, and each has passed away from our estimation as soon as higher degrees of improvement were attained, and better systems became visible."[11]

Turner painted a glowing portrait of the Saxon King Alfred, presenting him as an appropriate national hero. At great length (to a total of eleven chapters) he extolled the achievements and virtues of Alfred, who in his age was the world's "most beneficient luminary."[12]

For the Saxon language Turner had the highest praise. It was, contrary to those who had thought it a rude and barren tongue, "a very copious language . . . capable of expressing any subject of human thought." A study of principal authors from Shakespeare to Gibbon revealed a heavy preponderance of Saxon words, attesting to "the power of the Saxon language."[13]

Turner's history proved enormously popular and influential. It ran to seven editions by mid-century. His work provided source material and inspiration to politicians, statesmen, historians, publicists, who believed they saw all around them indications of England's superiority to all other nations.

In Turner's *History* one can find all the ingredients necessary for an explicitly racist interpretation of English history: the common Germanic origin of the English people; the exceptional courage and manliness of the Saxons, their predilection for freedom and the inherent excellence of their language and social institutions; the special affinity of the transmitted Saxon genius for science and reason; the inevitability of the ultimate triumph of a people so superbly endowed and directed by a kindly providence. These themes and their variations will be repeated and expanded upon by a host of commentators for the remainder of the century. Turner presented his account with a certain moderation and restraint; his successors will vie with each other in providing the most eloquent expression possible of Anglo-Saxon genius and achievement.

No one gloried more in the superiority of Germanic culture than Thomas Carlyle. An avid student of German literature and thought, admirer of Goethe and Schiller, he believed that England's continued excellence rested on those features of its Saxon past which promoted an aristocracy of race. Writing at the height of the industrial revolution, Carlyle maintained that it was the task of the new industrial leaders, "the Captains of the World," in the spirit of their Germanic ancestors, "Sons of the icy North," to assert themselves to restore aristocratic greatness to England: "Ye are most strong. Thor red-bearded, with his blue-son eyes, with his cheery heart and strong thunder hammer, he and you have prevailed. . . . What a Future; wide as the world, if we have the heart and heroism for it,–which, by Heaven's blessing, we shall."[14]

Industry and Protestantism, proceeding arm in arm, would assure England's supremacy. For Carlyle, like many Germanophiles, the Reformation became the touchstone by which European nations must be judged: "Protestant or not Protestant?" The question meant everywhere: "Is there anything of nobleness in you, O Nation, or is there nothing?" In his judgment, England nobly passed the test, for under Cromwell and his Puritans, "immensities of *dross* and crypto-poisonous matter" were burnt out to secure England's progress for centuries to come. Austria, Spain, Italy, France, Poland, all had been made offer of the Reformation, but all preferred "steady Darkness to uncertain new Light" and in consequence "all stars and heavenly lights" became veiled. "That is the doom passed upon them," concluded Carlyle.[15]

Undoubtedly the most highly regarded Anglo-Saxon scholar in the first half of the century was John Kemble, publisher of *Beowulf* (1833) and for many years editor of the *British and Foreign Review*. Kemble had studied Teutonic philology in Göttingen under Jacob Grimm and established himself as the leading English authority on pre-Norman social institutions. He approached his study with consummate seriousness. As he put it in the preface to his best known work, *The Saxons in England* (1849): "The subject is a grave and solemn one: it is the history of the childhood of our own age,–the explanation of its manhood." Kemble held that Englishmen had inherited the noblest portion of their being from the Saxons and it was they who had provided the principles which gave England its preeminence among the nations of Europe.

In outlining early Saxon forms of social organization, Kemble, drawing on the work of German historians, emphasized the importance of the Mark, the form of early Teutonic settlements allegedly introduced and brought to maturity in England by the Saxons. The Mark was considered in two senses, firstly, as a plot of land held in common on which freemen had settled for the purpose of cultivation; and, in a second and more important sense, as a community of families or households settled on community land, it was the fundamental base of all Teutonic society. The use of the land was dependent upon "the general will of the settlers, and could only be enjoyed under general regulations made by all for the benefit of all."[16] Thus the Mark, as a voluntary association of free men provided a basic framework of social organizations from which in time developed an entire structure of legal and political forms, uniquely Teutonic and Saxon in origin and underlying England's progression to imperial greatness.

Much of Kemble's understandably appealing theory on the significance of the Mark was derived from abstract philological speculation rather than from any solid historical evidence. Nevertheless his lead was enthusiastically taken up by later Anglo-Saxonists like Edward A. Freeman and William Stubbs, who went on to assert even more confidently the Germanic origin of English genius. It was not until the beginning of the twentieth century that the theory of a public land held in common as distinct from a royal demesne was finally and conclusively refuted by P. Vinogradoff and F. W. Maitland.[17]

In mid-century to mark the birth of King Alfred the Great (849), "the founder of our glory," a review entitled *The Anglo-*

Saxon was launched. Its object was a lofty one: "to harmonize the many members of the Anglo-Saxon race into the unity of Faith, and Hope and Love." Its pages were filled with eulogies to Alfred and praise of the "Angle-folk," the kindest and most loving, as well as the most powerful" of people. The jingoistic spirit which permeated the entire review is fairly represented by the opening stanza from a poem, "The Anglo-Saxon Race," contributed by the popular Victorian author, Martin F. Tupper:

> Stretch forth! stretch forth! from the south to the north,
> From the east to the west,—stretch forth! stretch forth!
> Strengthen thy stakes and lengthen thy cords,—
> The world is a tent for the world's true lords!
> Break forth and spread over every place
> The world is a world for the Saxon race.[18]

Within a year the publication ceased. Discriminating Anglo-Saxonists must have sighed with relief.

The second half of the century witnessed the apogee of Englishmen's confidence and pride of achievement. Encouraged by the apparently conclusive corroboration of other disciplines, Victorian historians allowed their enthusiasm for the Anglo-Saxon inheritance to reach unprecedented heights. Explicitly racial interpretations were frequently offered to explain cultural differences. Even such a sober scholar as Goldwin Smith, noted for his great impartiality, made use of biological and genetic categories to explain cultural variations. Thus in commenting on the difference between the Irish and English character he observed: "of the physical influences which affect the character and destiny of nations, the most important seems to be that of race." There is an unintended irony in his contrast of the freedom-loving Teuton and the despotic-leaning Kelt which would not be lost on his Irish reader: "The Teuton loves laws and parliaments, the Kelt loves a king. Even the highly civilized Kelt of France, familiar as he is with theories of political liberty, seems almost incapable of sustaining free institutions. After a moment of constitutional government he reverts, with a bias which the fatalist might call irresistible, to despotism in some form, whether it be that of a Bonaparte or that of a Robespierre."[19]

But for sheer exuberance and bluff prejudice in favor of Anglo-Saxonism, it would be difficult to match the rhetoric of one of the most popular writers of the day, Charles Kingsley. Clergyman, novelist and poet, from 1860 to 1869 he was professor of modern history at Cambridge. No one championed the cause of Anglo-Saxon Protestantism with greater vigor than Kingsley. It was beyond dispute, in Kingsley's mind, that the English were Teutons who turned aside from the great stream of Teutonic migrations and settled in Britain, "to till the ground in comparative peace, keeping unbroken the old Teutonic laws, unstained the old Teutonic faith and virtue. . . ." Their mission was now universal for "the welfare of the Teutonic race is the welfare of the world." The realization of their high destiny was not accidental, it was clearly a part of "the strategy of providence" for "in spite of all their sins, the hosts of our forefathers were the hosts of God."[20]

An equally vigorous and dramatic popularizer of history, and in his strong racial biases the complete Anglo-Saxonist, was James Anthony Froude. His 12-volume *History of England* (1865-70), written in a brilliant style, though much controverted proved a highly popular work and established his reputation as an historian. In Froude's judgment it was the Saxons' success in grafting on to their own hardy nature those things of value in the declining Western empire that explains the Anglo-Saxons' triumph, "that wonderful spiritual and political organization which remained unshaken for a thousand years." Froude lamented that in Reformation times the English and the Germans, "the two great streams of the Teutonic race, though separated by but a narrow ridge of difference, were unable to reach a common channel." The future, however, held the hope that their genius running side by side for centuries would converge at last.[21]

Froude's anti-Celtic bias was notorious. Writing at a time when the Irish Home Rule question constantly agitated English political life, Froude conveniently reduced the issue to one of racial characteristics. The Irish were by nature weak and should willingly submit to rule by their betters: "the ignorant and the selfish may be and are justly compelled for their own advantage to obey a rule which rescues them from their natural weakness . . . and those who cannot prescribe a law to themselves, if they desire to be free must be content to accept direction from others." England's continued dominance in Ireland was justified on the principle that "on the whole, and as a rule, superior strength is the equivalent of superior merit."[22]

Froude's Anglo-Saxon biases were if anything exceeded by another contemporary author and statesman, Sir Charles Wentworth Dilke. In 1866 he took a celebrated trip which brought him to Canada, the United States, New Zealand, Australia, and thence to Ceylon, India and Egypt, with the object of observing the colonies at first hand. Upon his return he published the widely acclaimed *Greater Britain: a Record of Travel.* Dilke was a racial imperialist of the first order. His book, which ran to numerous editions, was filled with reflections on the grandeur of "Saxendom"—the territories of the world formed in an English mold where "Alfred's laws and Chaucer's tongue" prevailed. In all countries visited Dilke observed a struggle of the "dear races" (peoples of Anglo-Saxon origin) against the "cheap races" (Irish, Chinese, Malays, Indians), but he was confident "that the dearer are, on the whole, likely to destroy the cheaper peoples, and that Saxendom will rise triumphant from the doubtful struggle." Dilke could anticipate the ultimate triumph of the Saxon with perfect moral equanimity, for to him it was clear that "the gradual extinction of the inferior races is not only a law of nature, but a blessing to mankind."[23]

Another distinguished writer who stressed the racial homogeneity of the English and called for imperial expansion was J. R. Seeley, professor of modern history at Cambridge from 1869 to his death in 1895. For Seeley the history of England was emphatically one of constant progress: "It is far greater now than it was in the eighteenth century; it was far greater in the eighteenth than in the seventeenth, far greater in the seventeenth than in the sixteenth. The prodigious greatness to which it has attained makes the question of its future infinitely important."

Seeley was optimistic that the British Empire would last longer than the great empires of the past which consisted of "congeries of nations held together by force." The bond of the British Empire was of a more vital kind, united by "blood and religion."[24]

A more formidable champion of Teutonic excellence was Edward A. Freeman, who established his considerable reputation as an historian through his six-volume *History of the Norman Conquest* (1867-76). Accepting without question the theory of the Aryans as the father race of western culture, Freeman believed a mission had been assigned to the three dominant Aryan nations, the Greek, the Roman and the Teuton, each in its own turn, "to be the rulers and the teachers of the world."[25]

That Englishmen were Teutons Freeman had not a doubt in the world: "I will assume that what is Teutonic in us is not merely one element among others, but that it is the very life and essence of our national being; that whatever else we may have in us, whatever we have drawn from those whom we conquered or from those who conquered us, is no co-ordinate element, but a mere infusion into our Teutonic essence; in a word, I will assume that Englishmen are Englishmen, that we are ourselves and not some other people." Freeman had absolute confidence that an unbroken cultural line extended from Victorian England to the Teutonic tribes of Germany: "I assume that, as we have had one national name, one national speech, from the beginning, we may be fairly held to have an unbroken national being. And when we find a Teutonic-speaking people in Britain living under the same political and social forms as the Teutonic-speaking peoples of the mainland, it is surely no very rash or far-fetched inference that the tongue and the laws which they have in common are a common possession drawn from a common source; that the island colony in short came itself, and brought its laws and language with it, from the elder mother-land beyond the sea." Englishmen, Freeman was at pains to emphasize, could also legitimately boast that their nation, beyond all doubt, was "the one among the great nations of modern Europe . . . which can claim for its political institutions the most unbroken descent from the primitive Teutonic stock." And alone among the political assemblies of the greater states of Europe, "the Parliament of England can trace its unbroken descent from the Teutonic institutions of the earliest times." Thus Englishmen might justly claim to have preserved more faithfully "than any of our kinsfolk the common heritage of our common fathers."[26]

Freeman's supreme assurance can be partially explained by his ready acceptance of the prevailing beliefs of the day, but more particularly by his confidence in the developing sciences of comparative philology and politics. On the former he once observed that "it has been placed on a firm basis, from which it is impossible to believe that it can ever be dislodged."[27] His firm convictions on the ethnic superiority and providential calling of the modern Anglo-Saxons led him at times to the extreme limits of racism. His disdain for the Irish and Negroes is illustrated by his clever but contemptuous comment to a friend during the course of an American visit in 1881, "This would be a grand land if only every Irishman would kill a negro, and be hanged for it."[28] In Freeman's vision only the continued dominance of Anglo-Saxon Protestants could assure the realization of America's full potential.

The influence of Freeman was evident in the work of his close friend, John Richard Green, one of the most influential historians of his generation. His *Short History of England* (1874), later expanded into *History of the English People* (1877-80), enjoyed an immense popularity. Green identified the beginnings of English history with "the landing of Hengist and his war-band . . . on the sands of Thanet." Thus from the fateful landing there unfolded the subsequent history of England with all its immense achievements. In Green's picturesque prose, "No spot in Britain can be so sacred to Englishmen as that which first felt the tread of English feet."[29] Green painted a glowing portrait of Alfred and, following Freeman, saw Anglo-Saxon institutions as fundamentally democratic.

The most careful and conscientious of nineteenth-century historians was undoubtedly William Stubbs. Regius professor of modern history at Oxford from 1866 to 1884, Bishop of Oxford from 1888, he had the greatest confidence of all in the Teutonic origins of English institutions: "[The English] are a people of German descent in the main constituents of blood character and language, but most especially . . . in the possession of the elements of primitive German civilisation and the common germs of German institutions."[30] Much influenced by German scholarship and his English predecessor John Kemble (whom he called "my pattern scholar"),[31] he believed that everything best in English society was Germanic in origin: "It is to Ancient Germany that we must look for the earliest traces of our forefathers, for the best part of almost all of us is originally German: though we call ourselves Britons, the name has only a geographic significance. The blood that is in our veins comes from German ancestors."[32]

Though less prone than many of his contemporaries to idealize early English history, he nevertheless strongly affirmed that the Anglo-Saxons, better than any other people, maintained and built upon the original genius of their Germanic forefathers. As he observed in his greatest work, *The Constitutional History of England* (1874-78), "If its [England's] history is not the perfectly pure development of Germanic principles, it is the nearest existing approach to such a development."[33]

Stubbs represents in his person the highest development of the dedicated Anglo-Saxonist. A staunch Christian who believed that England had a mission to bring liberty to the world, he interpreted its history as a providential unfolding of a divine plan. The study of history was accordingly, "next to theology itself, the most thoroughly religious training the mind can receive."[34] During his lifetime he witnessed the full flowering of modern nationalism and the spectacular expansion of British influence throughout the world. His scholarship was perhaps the best of a long line of Anglo-Saxonists reaching back to Camden and Verstegen, but like his compatriots, his patriotism colored his history.

The Anglo-Saxonism of most of the Protestant historians of the nineteenth century was relatively straightforward. The ambiguities of the myth were more evident in the work of the professedly Roman Catholic historian, Lord Acton, the most complex and stimulating liberal historian of the century. His position merits detailed consideration.

Chapter VI

ANGLO-SAXONISM AND ROMANISM

The Dilemma of Lord Acton

In his classic work, *The Whig Interpretation of History* (1931), Sir Herbert Butterfield expressed his astonishment "to what an extent the [English] historian has been Protestant, progressive, and whig, and the very model of the nineteenth-century gentleman." He went on to identify Lord Acton as the one in whom "the whig historian reached his highest consciousness."[1] The case of Lord Acton, the cosmopolitan scholar who, despite his Whiggism, professed that communion with the Roman Catholic Church was dearer to him than life, serves to illustrate the ambiguities sometimes present in English racial attitudes.

Acton's early background seems an unlikely one for a champion of Whiggism. He was born in Naples in 1834. His paternal grandfather was General Sir John Acton, an English adventurer who succeeded in winning the affection of the Queen of Naples and eventually becoming the Prime Minister under Ferdinand IV. His maternal grandfather, Duke Emeric Josef Dalberg, of ancient Hapsburg descent, became a French citizen during the Revolution, served as an aide to Talleyrand at the Congress of Vienna and later was created a French peer. An uncle, Charles Acton, was a Roman cardinal, and a chief advisor to the Pope. His father, Sir Ferdinand Richard, held office under the King of Naples, while his mother, Countess Marie Dalberg, an only child, was heir to the family estate at Herrinsheim, Bavaria.

At the age of three, upon the untimely death of his father, the infant John Acton succeeded to an English baronetcy, and with his German mother and guardian, was brought to his estate at Aldenham. In 1840 his mother married Lord Leveson, later the second Earl Granville and prominent liberal statesman. Acton's close familiarity with current English political values was guaranteed.

Acton's formal educational experience was as cosmopolitan as his origins. It began at a Catholic preparatory school near Paris, then under Félix Dupanloup, later an influential liberal bishop. On the completion of a year's study at the French school, he was enrolled at Oscott College, at the time directed by Nicholas Wiseman, the future cardinal. During his five years at Oscott, mainly through his own private reading, he developed a passionate interest in history, a subject poorly represented in a formal curriculum based mainly on the classics and traditional philosophy. The young boy longed for a private room where he could, in his own words, "build up a perfect library" and "study history very much."[2]

Following his years at Oscott, Acton continued his studies as a private student in Edinburgh, at the home of Dr. Logan, a former Vice-President of the College. He was tutored by a Presbyterian master, well versed in the classics. Formal academic demands were minimal and Acton had abundant time to pursue his developing interest in history. Edmund Burke soon became a special favorite. He was enthralled by Macaulay, and, on his own admission, read his works "at least four times."[3] His formation "as a regular schoolboy Whig" was well underway.[4] Though his infatuation with Macaulay was soon to be tempered by his German academic experience, the influence of Burke remained an abiding one for the remainder of his life.

Acton's two years at Edinburgh were seen by his parents as preparatory to his entering Cambridge. However, confronted with rejections from three Cambridge colleges on account of his religion–Acton will pointedly refer to this in 1895 in his Inaugural Lecture as Cambridge Regius Professor of Modern History–the boy's parents decided that he should go to Munich to study under Ignaz von Döllinger, the leading German Catholic historian. Acton was delighted by the prospects.

Acton resided with Döllinger and his studies were carefully supervised by his rigorous mentor. A remarkably close bond developed between the priest-scholar and his gifted student, and despite later intellectual strains always remained so. Döllinger made his splendid library resources available to his young protégé and set him to work at mastering the major continental historians. Ecclesiastical studies received a special emphasis. The as yet solidly ultramontane scholar cautioned against an excessive Macaulayism but encouraged a continued interest in Burke.

In the nineteenth century German universities were intensely alive and Munich was no exception. "The Munich Circle," comprising a group of progressive Catholic scholars, was recognized as the most advanced Catholic center in Europe. During vacation periods, Acton travelled widely with his mentor and made acquaintance with many leading European scholars.

Early in his German apprenticeship Acton was fired with a passion for the scientific study of history. German historians, led by Niebuhr and Ranke, had earlier revolutionized historical investigation. Through a more critical approach to sources many traditional interpretations were overturned. The study of the growth of church institutions and doctrines was particularly affected.

Döllinger impressed upon Acton the primacy of history in the study of theology. No longer could a serious scholar rest content with a systematic theology derived from medieval schoolmen notoriously ignorant of history. To think seriously about society was to think historically and in the world of history the law of development was the only constant. The God of History, it was firmly felt, was revealing Himself in a new way through German historians.

Acton's developing enthusiasm for scientific history was matched by a growing faith in liberalism as the highest expression of political morality. He had been introduced to liberal thought during his formative years in England, and in Germany became familiar with the work of continental Catholics who had espoused the liberal cause. In post-Revolutionary France, in particular, men such as Félicité de Lamennais and Count de Montalembert supported liberal political principles, but went on to argue eloquently that a free society was best guaranteed by a revived and reformed papacy. Although Lamennais' proposed program of reform was condemned by Gregory XVI in 1832, progressive German Catholic scholars came to believe that they were in an improved position to lead the Christian Church into the modern world. The stakes were high, for (it seemed to them) Protestantism was in a state of dissolution and many Protestants "were almost ready for re-entry into the Catholic Church."[5] It was manifestly Germany's sacred mission to once again lead the way to a revitalized Europe.

Acton's calling was also becoming clear. His work lay in England. The good things he had gathered in Germany must be shared with his fellow countrymen.

In the autumn of 1857 Acton returned to England, filled to the brim with historical learning and possessed of a high moral sense of a mission to be accomplished. For the next six years in the pages of the *Rambler* and its short-lived successor, the *Home and Foreign Review*, Acton devoted his energies to enlightening his readers on the true nature of freedom and politics. It was to prove the most productive period of his life.

He entered parliament in 1859 and in time became an intimate friend and admirer of William Gladstone. However, the world of practical politics proved totally uncongenial; his journalistic work remained primary. His output was impressive. "[P]erhaps in no organ of criticism in this country," remarked Matthew Arnold of the *Home and Foreign*, "was there so much knowledge, so much play of mind."[6]

In his political commentary Acton revealed himself as a complete Teutonist, but it was Teutonism with a sting for the Protestant reader. The roots of modern political liberty, he argued, were clearly Teutonic, but they grew out of a synthesis of a primitive Teutonic political system and Catholicism. In Acton's interpretation, the "Teutonic race received the Catholic ideas wholly and without reserve. . . . The nation was collectively Catholic, as well as individually." An understanding of this was as important for the future policy of the Church as for the State, since it was a plain fact "that the kind of liberty which the Church everywhere and at all times requires has been attained hitherto only in States of Teutonic origin."[7]

Acton maintained that the English Catholic was in a favored position to comprehend and defend the true nature of political freedom. It was, after all, Catholic principles that had inspired the British Constitution. It was England above all other States, which, "in the midst of its apostasy, and in spite of so much guilt towards religion," had preserved "the Catholic forms in its Church establishment more than any other Protestant nation, and the Catholic spirit in her political institutions more than any Catholic nation."[8] Indeed, Catholics "as the only permanent conservative element in the state," had a special duty to protect "the high parts of the constitution and its Christian character." In this work the great teacher was Edmund Burke, "the law and the prophets."[9]

In Acton's mind, England's success in maintaining a truly Teutonic-Catholic constitution was of paramount importance "in considering the missionary vocation of the English race in the distant regions it has peopled and among the nations it has conquered." No other country, he observed: "has preserved so pure the idea of liberty which gave the religion of old its power in Europe, and is still the foundation of the greatness of England."[10] By presenting a reformed Catholicism, together with a Teutonic political system, as the highest guarantor of freedom, Acton was confident he had neatly turned the tables on Protestant critics of Catholicism.

Acton, like all good Anglo-Saxonists, assumed the existence of an English race descended from a primitive Teutonic people. To question this was to him unthinkable. Thus in a review of H. T. Buckle's *History of Civilisation in England* he took the author severely to task for stating that "original distinctions of race are altogether hypothetical." He arrogantly rejected Buckle's position as "a great absurdity." In Acton's definitive judgment, "the same race of men preserves its character, not only in every region of the world, but in every period of history, in spite of moral as well as physical influences." Acton summarily dismissed the cautious Buckle as one who, "in his learned ignorance," endeavored to "degrade the history of mankind, and of the dealings of God with man, to the level of one of the natural sciences . . . and has stripped it of its philosophical, of its divine, and even of its human character and interest."[11] In Acton at least, restraint was not reckoned a Teutonic virtue.

On one decisive issue, it should be noted, Acton refused to go along with most of his Anglo-Saxon contemporaries, viz., nationalism. To Acton, the theory of nationalism which captivated so many nineteenth-century liberals represented a retrograde step in human history and augured ill for the future. As he commented in his brilliant essay on "Nationality" in the *Home and Foreign Review:* "A State which is incompetent to satisfy different races condemns itself; a State which labours to neutralize, to absorb, or to expel them, destroys its own vitality; a State which does not include them is destitute of the chief basis of self-government. The theory of nationality, therefore, is a retrograde step in history. . . . But nationality does not aim either at liberty or prosperity, both of which it sacrifices to the imperative necessity of making the nation the mould and measure of the State. Its course will be marked with material as well as moral ruin, in order that a new invention may prevail over the works of God and the interests of mankind."[12]

Acton's attempts to spark a Catholic Renaissance in England evoked more hostility than enthusiasm from almost all his co-religionists. A timid Catholic hierarchy, recently restored (1850) by a beleaguered papacy, could not comprehend how a movement born of German rationalism could aid the cause of religion. Acton, the antithesis of the submissive Catholic layman, totally perplexed them. In their minds he could best serve by silence.

Initially Acton was able to elicit the support of John Henry Newman, whose own orthodoxy was hardly above suspicion in the eyes of authority. Acton was attracted to Newman, through the latter's *Essay on the Development of Christian Doctrine* (1845), a work which, in Acton's words, "did more than any other book of his time to make his countrymen think historically, and watch the process as well as the result."[13] Acton had not yet fully developed his own theory of progress and was caught by Newman's insights. Later in life when he realized that Newman, in his theory, narrowly restricted the principle of development to the field of Catholic religious doctrine, and dismissed the idea of general progress as part of "the newspaper cant of the day," Acton was driven to categorize Newman's system of thought as "a school of Infidelity," for it appeared to deny God's providential rule in universal history.[14]

Alternating between despondency and reserved optimism, Acton, aided by his able editorial collaborator, Richard Simpson, pursued his work of educating reluctant Englishmen. The high point of the campaign for a more open and politically relevant Catholicism was reached in the autumn of 1863. Two important congresses were held at Malines and Munich. At the first gathering the great French liberal Catholic spokesman, Montalembert, presented the two principles of toleration and separation of Church and State as ones most appropriate for fostering freedom in a modern state. At the Munich Congress, a group of Catholic scholars, led by Döllinger, in effect claimed complete freedom of enquiry for Catholic intellectuals and denied the authority of Roman Congregations to control their investigations. Acton reported on both meetings in the *Home and Foreign*. He suggested that a new progressive age was dawning for Catholicism. Catholic Europe at last was about to accept its responsibilities for the direction of modern culture!

Before 1864 had run its course, Acton's hopes for a revitalized Catholicism collapsed. In three decisive statements Rome indicated that it had not the slightest intention of relaxing its total opposition to modern secular trends. Montalembert was reminded that his notions on religious liberty were identical to those of Lamennais and condemned by Gregory XVI in the encyclical *Mirari vos* (1832). In a brief addressed to the Archbishop of Munich, the Pope informed German scholars that they were obliged to follow all directives from the Holy See and were not free to pursue an independent line in theological and philosophical investigations. Finally, at the end of 1864, the *Syllabus of Errors*, with its harsh condemnations of modern civilization, appeared. To the plain reader it seemed that liberty itself stood condemned.

Acton saw no alternative to ending the *Home and Foreign*. He could not accept the principle put forth by the papacy and he believed it would be a scandal to continue the review in open opposition to the papacy. Rome, clearly, was committed to a new Counter Reformation, totally hostile to reform movements. Any effort to place Teutonic wisdom at the service of the Church was futile. Acton's failure remained with him as a crippling irritant for the remainder of his life, and his career as a productive scholar went into decline.

Ironically, at the very time Acton was imposing silence upon himself, Newman—who earlier in the *Rambler* had attempted a defense of the role of the laity in doctrinal matters only to have it delated to Rome as heretical—was feverishly responding, in his *Apologia Pro Vita Sua,* to Charles Kingsley's charge that the Catholic clergy were indifferent to truth for its own sake. Had Kingsley's wit matched his prejudices, and had he paid more careful attention to events going on under his nose, he would not have permitted Newman so easy a victory.

Prior to 1864 Acton was prepared to accept a reformed papacy as the keystone of European freedom, and to present ultramontanism as the loftiest expression of Catholicism. The increasing displays of Roman intolerance, however, convinced him that the papal institution he once hoped might be a guarantor of freedom was in reality a confirmed supporter of absolutism. The bitterness of his anti-papal invective increased and at times was reminiscent of emotional sixteenth-century Protestant reformers. In 1867, for example, in the course of a conversation on papal government with Odo Russell, the envoy of the British Government to the Vatican, Acton ended a long and eloquent condemnation with the passionate words: "I pray to God that I may live to see the whole of this [Papal] Fabric destroyed, and the Tiber flow with the blood of the massacred Priests." He further explained to the startled Russell: "The Church cannot be reformed and become what it ought [to be] and what I want it to be, unless it be destroyed and rebuilt."[15] Acton's Teutonic disdain for Rome hardly softened in subsequent years.

In the years following Vatican Council I, Acton turned away from ecclesiastical history and immersed himself more in post-Enlightenment thought. The twin ideas of the inevitability of human progress, and history as the unique manifestation of Divinity, became the center of his thinking.

Acton came to the conclusion that the key that unlocked the mystery of the movements of history was the theory of progress. Only in progress could one discover a justification of God's dealings with men. "My theory," he notes, "is that divine gov[ernment] is not justified without progress. There is no raison d'etre for the world."[16] In a revealing letter to Döllinger in 1882 he was more explicit: "there is a grand unity in the history of ideas—of conscience, of morality, and of the means of securing it. I venture to say that the secret of the philosophy of History lies there:—It is the only point of view from which one discovers a constant progress, the only one therefore which justifies the ways of God to man."[17]

It became Acton's firm conviction that the sacred task of detecting the path of progress, and identifying the obstacles in the way, fell to the historian. The historian was the guardian "of the conscience of mankind."[18] It was the historian's duty to identify immoral behavior in the past in order to guard against its recurrence in the future. The role of the historian was above all that of a moral judge, and, as he observed to a bemused audience in his "Inaugural Lecture" at Cambridge, "historical judgments have as much to do with hopes of heaven as public or private conduct."[19]

If the historian was to serve as "a supreme master, and a sovereign guide," it was to be presumed that his findings were definitive. Somehow Acton was able to convince himself that the science of history had, in his own day, attained the desired degree of critical excellence: "For men of equal competence, at a certain pitch of merit, there is no wide divergence possible. Their private theoretic opinions will remain. But their historical and moral judgment will be the same. The result is infallible, at a certain level."[20] A new infallibility was thus proposed against which the claims of the Pope appeared modest, an unexpected conclusion from the critic of absolute power.

Acton maintained to the end that his opinions proceeded from Catholic roots. It is far more plausible, as Herbert Butterfield suggests, "that they should be put down rather to his bias as a whig historian."[21] Like all his Whig contemporaries Acton had his eye on the present when condemning or praising the past. "Beware of too much explaining, lest we end by too much excusing," was one of his favorite counsels. The conviction that God was on the side of the Whig removed much of the burden of sympathetically striving to understand contrary positions.

A part of Acton remains an enigma. At times in his private notes we find questions being raised against some of his most cherished conclusions. Thus, for example, he notes that dogmatic liberalism may represent a threat to history: "Danger of liberalism to History. It has a dogmatic test. . . . History knows nothing of dogmatic right or wrong."[22] Though it is clear that the myth of primitive Teutonic freedom and its special relationship to English constitutional development exercised a profound influence on his thought, there is mention in his notes "that this legend has been overthrown."[23] His probing mind on occasion appeared to push him beyond his chosen liberal categories.

By the time of Acton's death in 1902 there were growing signs that the confident conclusions of Victorian scholars about England's racial inheritance and mission were more fragile than generally believed. New social and political conditions led to altered outlooks and prompted more cautious investigation. Nineteenth-century historians, however, might be forgiven their dogmatism when it is recognized to what a considerable degree their conclusions were supported by apparently compelling evidence from related areas of study. The sciences of philology and ethnology, in particular, appeared to confirm with incontrovertible proof the fondest convictions of patriotic historians.

Chapter VII

THE TESTIMONY OF SCIENCE

Philology and Ethnology

A powerful new auxiliary became available to the advocates of race as the key to national greatness with the rise of the science of philology. Philology, initially the science of language and literature but in time restricted to a study of linguistics, was established as a science by the painstaking work of such men as Sir William Jones, Jacob Grimm and Franz Bopp. Jones, a British orientalist and jurist, postulated the common ancestry of Sanskrit, Latin and Greek. His hypothesis, formulated in 1786, that similarities between these three languages and Persian, Celtic and German languages pointed to a common ancestral tongue which probably no longer existed made him the pioneer of modern philology. Further advances were made by German scholars like Franz Bopp and Jacob Grimm. In a work published in 1816, *On The Conjugational System of the Sanskrit Language in Comparison with that of the Greek, Latin, Persian, and Germanic Languages*, Bopp founded the science of comparative grammar. Grimm in his *German Grammar* (1819) demonstrated the regularity of the correspondence of consonants in Germanic and other languages associated with Sanskrit.

Initially the term "Aryan" (Sanskrit *arya*, noble) was the adjective applied to the division or family of languages which included Sanskrit, Zend, Persian, Greek, Latin, Celtic, Teutonic and Slavonic with their modern derivatives. In time "Aryan" was restricted to "Indo-European" (a term first used by Thomas Young, an English physicist, in an article in *The Quarterly Review*, in 1813). Gradually, the term "Indo-Germanic" worked its way into English usage and for a time was more popular than either Aryan or Indo-European. Its appeal to Anglo-Saxon enthusiasts is obvious.

The work of philologists attracted the attention of cultural nationalists. They were quick to identify those who spoke languages with Aryan roots as people who also possessed a common biological origin. Language became a test of race. Bishop Stubbs, for example, writing in the 1870s, observed that "language is by itself the nearest approach to a perfect test of national extraction. . . ."[1] Linguistic paleontologists rushed to work to establish the existence and place of origin of not just a common language but a common people. The myth of the Aryan race was born.

Though by the end of the century few serious scholars accepted the fallacious identification of race and language, in the intervening period scholars in England, Germany and France poured out a voluminous body of work postulated on the reality of an Aryan race. Writing in 1842, the highly respected English ethnologist, James Cowles Prichard, noted that it was "almost universally admitted [that the] collective body of the European nations [are] a great colony or a series of colonies of the Arian or the Indo-European race."[2]

By far the most successful publicist for the Aryan myth was Max Müller. Born in Germany, where he studied philology under Bopp, he came to England in 1846 with an established reputation as an orientalist and comparative philologist. In 1850 he was appointed deputy Taylorian professor of modern language at Oxford. His lectures on "The Science of Language" (1859-61), delivered at the Royal Institute in London, were widely attended and deeply impressed cultured Englishmen. With consummate eloquence, Müller spoke not only of an original Aryan language—a parent language from which English as a Teutonic language was obviously derived—but an Aryan people as well: "As sure as the six Romanic dialects point to an original home of Italian shepherds on the seven hills at Rome, the Aryan languages together point to an earlier period of language, when the first ancestors of the Indians, the Persians, the Greeks, the Romans, the Slavs, the Celts, and the Germans were living together within the same enclosures, nay under the same roof." Müller went on to propose their place or origin and the quality of their civilization: "before the ancestors of the Indians and Persians started for the south, and the leaders of the Greek, Roman, Celtic, Teutonic and Slavonic colonies marched towards the shores of Europe there was a small clan of Aryans, settled probably on the highest elevation of Central Asia, speaking a language, not yet Sanskrit or Greek or German, but containing the dialectical germs of all; a clan that had advanced to a state of agricultural civilization; that had recognized the bonds of blood, and sanctioned the bonds of marriage; and that invoked the Giver of Light and Life in heaven by the same name which you may still hear in the temple of Benares, in the Basilicas of Rome, and in our own churches and cathedrals."[3]

Englishmen understandably took pride in their ancient racial inheritance as outlined by Müller. However as time went on Müller more and more came to have serious reservations about his earlier theories and ended by totally rejecting the identification of race and language. As he dramatically stated it in 1888: "To me an ethnologist who speaks of Aryan race, Aryan blood, Aryan eyes and hair, is as great a sinner as a linguist who speaks of a dolichocephalic dictionary or a brachycephalic grammar. It is worse than a Babylonian confusion of tongues—it is downright theft. We have made our own terminology for the classification of languages; let ethnologists make their own for the classification of skulls, and hair, and blood."[4]

Müller's courageous retraction did little to stem the growth of a type of thinking which identified national genius with race and language. The myth of the Aryan race continued to be circulated and was used everywhere to support theories of Nordic superiority. Even Sir E. B. Tylor, a cultural anthropologist of the highest distinction, who criticized those who carelessly took "language and race as though they went always and exactly together," went on to make use of categories like, "our Aryan ancestors . . . lower races . . . high and low nations."[5]

Elitist racial theories stressing Nordic superiority received further confirmation from the new sciences of ethnology and anthropology (in nineteenth-century usage the two terms were frequently synonymous). Beginning in the eighteenth century, pioneers like the Swedish botanist Carl von Linneaus, the French naturalist Comte de Buffon and the German physician Johann Friedrich Blumenbach attempted to classify men principally on the basis of biological differences. As evolutionary thinking came into vogue in the nineteenth century, the work of the early pioneers was expanded and by mid-century it was commonplace among ethnologists and anthropologists to classify men into distinct racial groups on the basis of such physical characteristics as skin and hair color, shape of skull or pelvis, stature, form of nose and so on. Few limited themselves to mere classification; most went on to assert a vital connection between physical characteristics and moral and intellectual qualities.

The practice of associating intellectual and cultural superiority with physical characteristics reached its most dramatic development in the science of phrenology, the study of the conformation of the skull as an indicator of mental ability and character. It was the German anatomist Franz Joseph Gall who pioneered the study. The title of the work which established his reputation captures the essence of his thesis: *The Anatomy and Psychology of the Nervous System in General and the Skull in Particular, with Observations How Moral and Intellectual Predispositions of Men and Animals Can be Recognized through the Configuration of Their Heads* (1810-19). A generation later the Swedish scientist Andreas Retzius introduced the concept of the cephalic index, a percentage ratio based on a comparison of the length to the breadth of the human skull, which was presumed to provide a quantitative measurement of human potential. Thus dolichocephaly (long-headedness, an index less than 80) was postulated as being characteristic of the Germanic people and indicated high intellectual capacity, just as brachycephaly (short- or broad-headedness, an index more than 80) was typical of inferior or retarded people.

Gradually the use of the cephalic index as an analytical tool became commonplace among scholars. So pervasive was its influence that even those who had come to reject the validity of the Aryan race concept still resorted to the cephalic index as a valuable aid for interpreting human development. Thus Isaac Taylor, a leading English philologist, who categorically dismissed any identity between an Aryan language and a specific race "as a mere figment, wholly contrary to the evidence," went on to explain complex social and religious divisions in terms of the index: "The dolichocephalic Teutonic race is Protestant, the brachycephalic Celto-Slavic race is either Roman Catholic or Greek Orthodox. In the first, individualism, wilfullness, self-reliance, independence, are strongly developed; the second is submissive to authority and conservative in instincts."[6]

The pages of learned reviews, such as the *Journal of the Ethnological Society* and its rival *The Anthropological Review*, bristled with discussions over the physical and psychological differences which marked the Teuton off from the Celt, the Negro, the Eskimo. Pleas for greater caution and sobriety from scientists like T. H. Huxley went unheeded.

At a time when Irish Home Rule dominated politics, anti-Irish prejudice exploded under the guise of scientific observation. On one occasion Dr. John Beddoe, President of the Anthropological Society of London, took Huxley severely to task for denying "that there is sufficient proof of the existence of any difference whatever, except that of language, between Celts and Teutons."[7]

Dr. Beddoe, whose avowed aim in his best known work, *The Races of Britain*, was "to lay a sure foundation . . . and reject unsound material," nevertheless maintained that by basing the study of racial differentiation on two principal factors, color of hair and color of iris (his "index of nigrescence"), trustworthy conclusions about ethnic origin could be established. Thus he concluded that in his own day in the greater part of England, "Anglo-Saxon or Scandinavian blood . . . amounts to something like a half."[8] It went without saying that it was the better half.

At the end of the century established anthropologists were still publishing works filled with racist preconceptions. A. H. Keane in his *Man: Past and Present* (1900) asserted that the Saxon race, now dominant in the United States, Canada, Australia, and South Africa had sufficient numbers "to ensure the future control of human destinies." The Saxon's temperament, in Keane's view, made him a natural leader, "stolid and solid, outwardly abrupt but warm-hearted and true, haughty and even overbearing through an innate sense of superiority, yet at heart sympathetic and always just, hence a ruler of men."[9]

Another anthropologist, N. C. Macnamara, in his *Origin and Character of the British People* reasserted every popular racial dogma of the day. Race, according to Macnamara, had a determining influence on all personal and social characteristics, and the shape of the skull was "the best and only reliable test of race." The present ascendancy of England was directly attributable to the descent of its people "from the grand old Aryan race." The maintenance of unity and integrity of the Teutonic race was of paramount importance, for upon it depended "the progress and the freedom of the human family." In seeking to identify the genuine Teuton, Macnamara could offer no better examples than "the present Emperor of Germany, his illustrious father and grandfather, and Frederick the Great."[10]

In the continuing chorus of racial rhetoric throughout the latter half of the nineteenth century, one supporting voice was conspicuously absent, that of Sir Charles Darwin. Despite the popularity of his evolutionary theory among some racial interpreters, Darwin himself exercised the greatest caution in applying evolutionary thought to an explanation of the moral and intellectual development of men. Contrary to most of his contemporaries, he rejected the idea that progress was an invariable rule. As he concluded in his sequel to *The Origin of Species*, *The Descent of Man:* "It is very difficult to say why one civilized nation rises, becomes more powerful, and spreads more widely, than another; or why the same nation progresses more quickly at one time than at another. We can only say that it depends on an increase in the actual number of the population, on the number of the men endowed with high intellectual and moral faculties, as well as on their standard of excellence. Corporeal structure appears to have little influence, except so far as vigour of body leads to vigour of mind."[11]

Darwin's hesitancy was atypical of his age. But the caution of scientists like Darwin and Huxley exerted its influence. As the nineteenth century ran its course, other voices were heard questioning the racial assumptions of the day. There were unmistakable signs that Anglo-Saxonism as a vital ideology binding together Englishmen and justifying their activities was on the wane.

Chapter VIII

THE DISINTEGRATION OF AN IDEOLOGY

Writing at the end of the nineteenth century, the British literary and social critic, John MacKinnon Robertson, lamented that the connection between liberty and Teutonic virtue was so firmly held in modern literature that its reconsideration seemed almost hopeless.[1] Yet Robertson himself, with considerable success, went on to offer a sweeping reconsideration in which he exposed many of the absurdities implicit in current racial interpretations of English and German history.[2] Within a generation of his initial observations most of the racial shibboleths that had been so widely accepted were no longer tenable by any scholarly standard.

The pursuit of the homeland of an alleged Aryan race, an enterprise that had occupied so many scholars in the previous century, was finally seen as a fruitless search provoked by a false identification of language and peoples. The concept of an identifiable Teutonic race, a race of outstanding character and possessed of an essentially democratic social organization, came to be rejected as an historical anachronism. A recent authority judged the early Saxon immigrants as, "pagan, non-literate and barbaric, heroes of a northern society so disorganized that they had little conception of national, racial or political loyalties."[3] The witenagemot, for centuries proposed as an ancient Teutonic popular assembly, the prototype of the English parliament, was judged, in the words of F. W. Maitland, "a small aristocratic body, tending always to become more aristocratic."[4] Equally, Magna Charta, since the seventeenth century lauded as the great charter of English freedoms, came to be seen for what it was, an essentially feudal document with slight relevance for later societies. Sir Herbert Butterfield relates in his Stenton Lecture of 1968, how, as a young student, it came to him as a thrill to learn that the myth of Magna Charta was overthrown early in the twentieth century.

The most durable and pervasive racial myth of all undoubtedly was the belief that somehow modern Englishmen were one in blood with the ancient Teutons (who presumably were also of a pure blood line) and that their relatively unmixed origin from superior stock explained and justified their national and imperial successes. However twentieth-century scholarship has dealt severely with the concept of racial purity. With more objective study it became abundantly clear that the Teutonic invaders who established themselves in Britain from the fifth century onward were simply one addition among many others to the ethnic composition of its inhabitants. Professor N. K. Chadwick, a recognized modern authority on the subject, has expressed her personal belief that "the predominant element in the population of England is Celtic."[5] The work of craniologists and ethnologists who presumed to establish scientifically the relative racial purity of Anglo-Saxons came to be seen as based not on evidence but on wishful thinking. As Karl Pearson, the British biometrician and anthropologist observed in 1920: "What we know historically on folk wanderings, folk-mixings, and folk-absorptions have undoubtedly been going on for hundreds of thousands of years, of which we know only a small historical fragment . . . it is hopeless to believe that anthropometric measurements of the body or records of pigmentation are going to help us to a science of the psychophysical characteristics of man which will be useful to the state."[6]

The reasons for the rapid disintegration of a set of beliefs that had been held with such unshakeable conviction by men of considerable intellectual stature are complex. The most general reason is related to the loss of confidence on the part of many in the predestined triumph of nationalistic and imperialistic values. The easy optimism of nineteenth-century liberals seemed scarcely warranted to a new generation experiencing the division of Europe into several armed camps jealously eyeing each other and finally culminating in a general world war. Again, the earlier confidence of English and German scholars that the source of human dignity and political independence flowed in a direct line from primitive Germanic sources appeared incredible to the serious observer of post-Bismarckian Germany. In particular the increasingly strident racist dogmas gaining favor in Germany indicated the threat to human freedom inherent in the exploitation of race for political ends. In England, the growing awareness that Kaiser Wilhelm's expansionist aspirations posed a serious threat to British imperial interest dampened enthusiasm for the German association. Not much was heard in England about Teutonic excellence after World War I. Germany, for its own part, aspiring to be a great world power, began to parade itself as the exclusive recipient and principal protector of the ancient Teutonic inheritance.

Finally, shifts took place within the world of scholarship. The dogmatic confidence of the nineteenth century gave way to a greater appreciation of the subjective element in all scientific and historical interpretation; the prejudices born of patriotism were more clearly recognized. But especially the increased emphasis given to economic factors in explaining the genesis and growth of political and social institutions, rendered suspect earlier interpretations emphasizing racial transmission. The work of scholars had become less dramatic but perhaps more objective. In such an atmosphere exaggerated national myths fared ill.

As has been seen myths of origin played an important role in the historic march of England from rude beginnings to nationhood and empire. The myth of Trojan origins, during its period of ascendancy, was found serviceable to most Englishmen. The racial element, while present, was not overly stressed. The myth of Anglo-Saxonism, however, from its beginning, emphasized exclusivity. Taking form during the Reformation period, when England was on the way to becoming the first European nation-state, from the first it gave prominence to the essentially Saxon and Protestant nature of the English political and religious community. From the seventeenth century onward, as England moved from nation to empire, belief in the inherently superior quality of the Englishman's character and his predestined civilizing mission grew accordingly. Yet, the tendency to ascribe to ancient Saxon ancestors the social organization of later times and to exaggerate their political progressiveness served to conceal their truly significant cultural achievements in art and literature.

On balance, the myth of Anglo-Saxonism served England's national purposes well. Belief in their racial supremacy encouraged visionary Englishmen to look beyond their shores to other continents and proceed to build a great world empire to support a vibrant domestic society. Still, little attention was given to the cruel toll exacted from the multitude of victims left in its wake, the blacks, the Irish, the exploited indigenous peoples of the colonies. The idea of mission seemed to justify everything. Joseph Conrad gave revealing expression to the moral ambiguity at the core of the imperialist stance in a haunting passage in his *Heart of Darkness:* "The conquest of the earth, which mostly means the taking it away from those who have a different complexion or slightly flatter noses than ourselves, is not a pretty thing when you look into it too much. What redeems it is the idea only. An idea at the back of it; not a sentimental pretence but an idea; and an unselfish belief in the idea—something you can set up, and bow down before, and offer a sacrifice to ____."[7]

It is not accidental that the fullest expression of the national myth coincided with the highest realization of national aspirations, nor that its disintegration was simultaneous with England's decline as a great power. Its continuing strength was undoubtedly manifested in the nation's stouthearted determination to defend itself against odds in World War II; yet, there is a terrible irony in England's need to rally against an offensive tyranny of the most violently racial form perpetrated by the self-proclaimed keepers of the Teutonic conscience.

The events of the twentieth century which have so reduced England's (and indeed Europe's) international position have left the myth of Anglo-Saxonism badly tarnished. Its educated defenders today are few, though it lives on as part of folk prejudice. Its principles still surface whenever, for example, the present-day champions of English cultural and racial supremacy, the members of the National Front, hold a public rally; or with greater subtlety, when the Prime Minister publicly expresses concern lest traditional English culture be "swamped" by alien influence and calls for "a clear prospect of an end to immigration."[8] Yet it is doubtful if either the ethno-centrism of a neo-Facist populist movement or the exasperations of a Tory leader faced with intractable domestic problems can do much to revive a spent myth which has outlived its political usefulness.

NOTES

Where unspecified, London is the place of publication.

CHAPTER I

1. Halvdan Koht, "The Dawn of Nationalism in Europe," *American Historical Review,* 52 (Jan., 1947), p. 271.
2. *The History of the British Kings,* trans., Lewis Thorpe (Harmondsworth, Penguin, 1966), p. 51.
3. Gildas in his *De Excidio et Conquesta Britanniae* (c. 550) presented a condensed and sometimes incoherent reconstruction of the Roman and Anglo-Saxon conquests. The *Historia Brittonum* (c. 900), generally assigned to Nennius, is a very brief, semi-legendary account of the Britons. Both works are cited by Geoffrey. The far more reliable *Historia Ecclesiastica Gentes Anglorum* (731) by Bede was used by Geoffrey but it has little on the Britons. In a recent article in *Speculum,* Geoffrey Ashe argues with some cogency that "an unknown source of some kind remains possible." ("A Certain Very Ancient Book," April, 1981), p. 301.
4. Bede makes no mention of Trojan origins, suggesting that the tradition was not accepted in Britain in his time.
5. *Aluredi Beverlacensis Annales,* ed., Thomas Hearne (Oxford, 1716), p. 2.
6. *Annales,* p. 76.
7. *Itinerarium Cambrensis,* VI Rolls Series, Book I, Ch. v, ed., J. F. Dimock (1868), 58-59.
8. *The History of William of Newburgh,* trans., J. Stevenson, *The Church Historians of England,* IV, part I, Preface (1856).
9. See G. H. Gerould, "King Arthur and Politics," *Speculum,* II (Jan., 1927), 33-51.

10. See R. H. Fletcher, *The Arthurian Material in the Chronicles* (New York, 1966), pp. 191ff., 279ff.
11. R. S. Loomis, "Edward I, Arthurian Enthusiast," *Speculum*, XXVIII (Jan., 1953), 114-27.
12. *The Annals of Waverly*, cited in G. Ashe, *The Quest for Arthur's Britain* (1968), pp. 99-100.
13. See V. M. Lagorio, "The Evolving Legend of St. Joseph of Glastonbury," *Speculum*, XLVI, 1971.
14. Loomis, pp. 121-22.
15. See Arthur Jocelyn, *Awards of Honour* (1956), p. 17.
16. Ashe, *Arthur's Britain*, p. 12.
17. See Sydney Anglo, "The British History in Early Tudor Propaganda," *Bulletin of the Johns Rylands Library*, 44 (1961-62), 21-44.
18. See Eugene Vinaver, "Sir Thomas Malory," *Arthurian Literature in the Middle Ages*, ed. R. S. Loomis (Oxford, 1959).
19. *The Works of Sir Thomas Malory*, ed. E. Vinaver (1954), Preface, p. xvi.
20. Cited in John Speed, *The History of Great Britain* (1614), p. 164.
21. Cited in John Leland, *De Rebus Britannicis Collectanea*, ed., T. Hearne (1770), p. 196.
22. See Howell T. Evans, *Wales and the War of the Roses* (1915), p. 7.
23. *Historia Regis Henrici Septimi*, ed., James Gairdner, *Memorials of King Henry VII* (1858), pp. 9-11.
24. *Chronicles* (1809), p. 428.
25. *The Historie of the Raigne of King Henry the Seventh*, (1622), p. 18.
26. T. D. Kendrick, *British Antiquity* (1970), p. 38.
27. See E. A. Greenlaw, *Studies in Spenser's Historical Allegories* (1932), p. 40.
28. R. Koebner, " 'The Imperial Crown of this Realm': Henry VIII, Constantine The Great and Polydore Vergil," *Bulletin of the Institute for Historical Research*, XXVI (1953), 40.
29. Koebner, p. 31.
30. See Denys Hay, *Polydore Vergil* (Oxford, 1952), p. 9.
31. *Polydore Vergil's English History*, from an early 16th century translation, ed., Sir Henry Ellis (1846), pp. 29, 33.
32. Vergil, p. 30.
33. Vergil, p. 38.
34. Vergil, p. 122.
35. Koebner, p. 36.
36. In 1536 Leland wrote a brief response entitled *Antiquarii Codrus, Sive Laus et Defensio Gallofridi Arturii Monumetensus contra Poly-*

dorum Virgilium. This was expanded in 1544 in *Assertio Inclytissmii Arturii, Regis Britanniae.*
37. *The Assertion of K. Arthure,* a sixteenth century translation by Richard Robinson, ed., Christopher Middleton, in *The Famous Historie of Chinon of England* (1925), p. 53.
38. Leland, p. 17.
39. Leland, p. 86.
40. Leland, pp. 89-90.
41. *Select Works of John Bale* (Parker Society, 1849), p. 8.
42. The *Defensio* was written c. 1553 but not published until 1573.
43. See Kendrick, pp. 87-89.
44. Cited in Hay, p. 159.
45. See Hay, Ch. V; McKisack, *Medieval History in the Tudor Age* (Oxford, 1971), pp. 98-102. For his general influence see C. L. Kingsford, *English Historical Literature in the 15th Century* (1913).
46. *The Pastyme of People* (1811), p. 7.
47. Rastell, p. 106.
48. Kendrick, p. 41.
49. See Greenlaw, pp. 42-50.
50. McKisack, p. 152.
51. *Britannia,* trans., Edmund Gibson (1722), pp. 4-6.
52. See F. J. Levy, "The Making of Camden's Britannia," *Bibliotheque d'humanisme et Renaissance* XXVI (1964).
53. *Britannia,* p. 15.
54. *Britannia,* p. 183.
55. See R. F. Brinkley, *Arthurian Legend in the Seventeenth Century* (1932), Ch. 1; A. E. Parsons, "The Trojan Legend in England," *Modern Language Review,* XXIV (July, 1929), 402ff.
56. *Works,* ed., J. Hebel, IV, song X (1903), 206.
57. *Works,* p. 207.
58. Cited in Oliver Elton, *Michael Drayton* (New York, 1966), p. 112.
59. *A Historie of the Warres* (1607), p. 3.
60. Ayscu, p. 4.
61. Cited in George S. Gordon, *The Discipline of Letters* (Oxford, 1946).
62. *The History of Great Britaine under the Conquests of Ye Romans, Saxons, Danes and Normans* (1614), p. 166. Venus, as mother of Aeneas, was accordingly great-grandmother of Brutus.
63. Speed, p. 316.
64. Speed, p. 317.
65. *The History of the World* (1614).
66. *The Annales or General Chronicle of England* (1615), p. 6.

67. Cited in C. H. Firth, *Essays Historical and Literary* (Oxford, 1938), p. 70.
68. *Hypercritica: or a rule of Judgement, for Writing or Reading our History* (1722), pp. 205-06.
69. Bolton, p. 206.
70. Bolton, p. 212.
71. Silas, Taylor, *The History of Gavel-kind* (1663), p. 83.
72. *The Destruction of Troy*, "Prologue," (1679).
73. *The History of the Nine Worthies of the World* (1687), pp. 146-47.
74. Cited in C. E. Ward, *The Life of John Dryden* (1961), p. 250.
75. See Ian R. Jack, *Augustan Satire* (Oxford, 1942), p. 5.

CHAPTER II

1. *Ecclesiastical History of the English Nation* (Everyman, 1954), p. 5.
2. E. N. Adams, *Old English Scholarship in England* (New Haven, 1917), p. 111.
3. See C. E. Wright, "The Dispersal of the Monastic Libraries and the Beginnings of Anglo-Saxon Studies," *Transactions of the Cambridge Bibliographical Society*, I (1951), 208-37.
4. Wright, p. 211.
5. Bale believed that the Reformation was a purifying movement ending a thousand-year-rule by Antichrist.
6. July, 1560. Reprinted in "Communications," *Cambridge Antiquarian Society*, III (1864-1876), 157.
7. *Illustrium Majoris Britanniae Scriptorum* (1548); revised and expanded to *Scriptorum Illustrium Majoris Britanniae . . . Catalogus* (1557-59).
8. *The Image of bothe Churches after the most wonderfull and heavenlie Revelacion of Saint John* (1550), reprinted in *Select Works of John Bale*, ed., H. Christmas (Parker Society, 1849), p. 251.
9. Bale, pp. 502-03.
10. Bale, p. 564.
11. *Examinations of Anne Askewe*, reprinted in *Select Works*, p. 188.
12. Bale, *Examinations*, p. 188; *The Pageant of Popes*, trans., by John Studley of *Acta Romanorum Pontificum* (1574), fol. 23.
13. *The Actes of English Votaryes* (1548), fol. 23.
14. *The Lives of those eminent Antiquarians, John Leland, Thomas Hearne, and Anthony à Wood.*, ed., W. Huddesford, I (Oxford, 1772), pp. 9-10.
15. John Bale, *The Laboryouse Journey and Serche of Johan Leylande* (1549), fol. C.

16. Bale, *Journey*, fol. 54.
17. *Actes and Monuments* (1841), p. 237.
18. Foxe, p. 250.
19. Foxe, p. 193.
20. Cited in H. Kohn, *The Idea of Nationalism* (New York, 1945), pp. 625-26.
21. *The History of the Church of England*, compiled by Venerable Bede, Englishman (Antwerp, 1565), fol. 3.
22. Parker, *D.N.B.*, XV (1921-22), p. 260.
23. John Strype, *Life and Acts of Matthew Parker* (1711), p. 55.
24. *The Gospels of the Fower Evangelistes* (1571).
25. See J. F. Mozley, *John Foxe and His Book* (1940), pp. 80-81.
26. *Gospels*, fols. aii, cii, aiii.
27. *Correspondence of Matthew Parker*, eds., Bruce and Perowne (Cambridge, Parker Society, 1853), p. 425.
28. See McKisack, *Medieval History*, Chapter 11.
29. See Robin Flower, "Laurence Nowell and the Discovery of England in Tudor Times," *Proceedings of the British Academy*, XXI (1935), pp. 47-73.
30. See Adams, *Old English Scholarship*, p. 29, n. 2.
31. For a full transcript of the fascinating interview see McKisack, pp. 81-82.
32. Cited in Leon Poliakov, *The Aryan Myth* (Brighton, 1974), p. 77.
33. See R. F. Jones, *The Triumph of the English Language* (1953), pp. 216-18.
34. *Tacitus on Britain and Germany*, trans., H. Mattingly (Harmondsworth, Penguin, 1948), 4, p. 103.
35. J. M. Wallace-Hadrill, for example, has written: "The *Germania* is not only an unsafe guide to future Germanic society, it also affords no solid ground for generalization about Germanic society at large of the historians own time." *Germanic Kingship* (Oxford, 1971), p. 2.
36. Cited in Poliakov, p. 82.
37. "An appeal to the Ruling Class of German Nationality," *Reformation Writings of Martin Luther*, trans., B. L. Woolf I (1952), 192-93.
38. Cited in Poliakov, p. 84.
39. *Philadelphus; or, a defence of Brutes, and the Brutan History* (1593), p. 97.
40. *Britannia*, p. xxx.
41. Camden, pp. xxix; 82-86.
42. *Remaines Concerning Britain* (1657), pp. 20-21, 12, 18, 13.
43. Cited in S. Kliger, *Goths in England* (Cambridge, Mass., 1952), pp. 248-49.

44. *A Restitution of Decayed Intelligence in Antiquities Concerning the Most Noble and Renowned English Nation* (1673), p. 47.
45. Verstegen, pp. 2, 47-48.
46. Verstegen, pp. 203-04.
47. Verstegen, pp. 210-13.
48. *Remaines*, p. 25.
49. *A Saxon Treatise Concerning the Old and New Testament* (1623), Preface.
50. *Logonomia Anglica* (1619), p. 247.
51. *Saxon Treatise*, Preface.

CHAPTER III

1. Cited in F. S. Fussner, *The Historical Revolution* (1962), p. 95.
2. *History of Great Britaine* (1614), pp. 287-289.
3. See H. M. Cam, "Magna-Carta–Event or Document?" Selden Society Lecture, July 7, 1965.
4. See E. Evans, "Of the Antiquity of Parliaments in England," *History*, XXIII (1938), 209.
5. Philip Styles, "Politics and Historical Research in the Early Seventeenth Century," *English Historical Scholarship in the Sixteenth and Seventeenth Centuries*, ed., Levi Fox (1956), p. 60.
6. Cited in V. H. Galbraith, "The Modus Tenendi Parliamentum," *Journal of the Warburg and Courtauld Institutes*, 16 (1953), p. 81.
7. F. W. Maitland, Introd., *The Mirror of Justice*, ed., W. J. Whittaker (Selden Society, 1895), p. xxxviii.
8. Horn, pp. 6, 7, 155.
9. Horn, Introd., p. x.
10. *De Laudibus Legum Angliae* (1741), pp. 30, 33-34.
11. Cited in J. E. C. Hill, *Puritanism and Revolution* (1958), p. 66.
12. Cited in John E. Adair, *A Life of John Hampden* (1976), p. 2.
13. *St. Edward's Ghost: or, Anti-Normanisme. Being a Patheticall Complaint and Motion in the behalfe of our English Nation against her grand (yet neglected) grievance, Normanisme* (1647), pp. 3, 4.
14. Hare, pp. 10-11, 12-13.
15. Hare, pp. 13-14, 19-21, 23.
16. *An Historicall Discourse of the Uniformity of the Government of England* (1647), pp. 47, 53.
17. *For the Sacred Law of the Land* (1652), pp. 65, 55, 216.
18. Cited in L. F. Solt, *Saints in Arms* (1959), p. 73.
19. *A Voice from Heaven to the Commonwealth of England* (1652), pp. 19-20.

20. Cited in J. F. Wilson, *Pulpit in Parliament* (Princeton, 1969), p. 201.
21. *A Discourse of the Nationall Excellencies of England* (1658), pp. 15, 245-46.
22. Hawkins, pp. 246, 248-49.
23. J. E. C. Hill, *The English Revolution 1640* (1955), p. 57.
24. Thomas Pugh, *British and Outlandish Prophecies* (1658), cited in Arise Evans, *A Rule from Heaven*, pp. 24-25 (1659).
25. E. W. Kerby, "The Reconcilers and the Restoration," *Essays in Modern English History* (Cambridge, Mass., 1941), p. 51.
26. *English Historical Document 1660-1671*, VII (1953), p. 57.
27. J. H. Plumb, *The Growth of Political Stability in England 1675-1725* (1967), pp. 32-33.
28. See D. C. Douglas, "The Norman Conquest and British Historians," David Murray Foundation Lecture (Glasgow, 1946), p. 9.
29. *Divi Britannici* (1675), p. 105.
30. Churchill, pp. 106, 187, 362.
31. In a royal dedication to a new Latin translation of John Spelman's *Life of Alfred* (1678).
32. *The History of Britain. Complete Prose Works of John Milton*, V, 1 (New York, 1971), 2, 3, 8.
33. Charles Firth, *Essays Historical and Literary* (1958), p. 74.
34. Milton, pp. 3, 183.
35. Milton, pp. 258, 259.
36. Cited in Firth, p. 71, n. 2.
37. Cited in J. E. C. Hill, *Milton and the English Revolution* (1977), p. 114.
38. See G. F. Sensabaugh, *The Grand Whig Milton* (Stanford, 1952), Ch. V.
39. Adams, *Old English Scholarship*, p. 74.

CHAPTER IV

1. Plumb, *Political Stability*, p. 2.
2. J. P. Kenyon, *The Stuarts* (1977), p. 159.
3. *The Work of Sir William Temple*, II (1731), 553, 556.
4. Temple, II, 218-219.
5. *Anglia Libera* (1701), pp. 111, 110, 129.
6. *Toland*, pp. 13, 14.
7. Cited in J. E. C. Hill, *The Century of Revolution 1603-1714* (1974), p. 256.
8. *The True-born Englishman* (1706), pp. 11, 12.
9. Defoe, p. 23.

10. *Jure Divino*, Book IX (1706), pp. 205, 206 N., A.
11. *A Discourse of the Contests and Dissentions Between the Nobles and the Commons in Athens and Rome* (Oxford, 1701), ed., F. H. Ellis (1967), pp. 118; 87.
12. 'Abstract of the History of England', *Prose Works of Jonathan Swift*, ed., T. Scott (1897-1908), 225.
13. *Camden's Britannia* (1722), Preface.
14. *The Critical History of England*, I (1728), 23-24, 25.
15. *An Introduction to the Old English History* (1684). See J. G. A. Pocock, 'The Brady Controversy', *The Ancient Constitution and the Feudal Law* (Cambridge, 1957), Ch., viii.
16. Cited in Kliger, *Goths*, p. 8.
17. On the controversy see Isaac Krammick, "Augustan Politics and English Historiography," *History and Theory* 6 (1967), 33-56.
18. *Remarks on the History of England* (1747), pp. 51, 52, 53.
19. Bolingbroke, p. 54.
20. *Letters Concerning the English Nation*, ed., Charles Whibley (1926), pp. 49, 47, 50.
21. See his article in *Dictionnaire Philosophique*, "Franc ou Franq, France, Francois, Français."
22. *The Spirit of the Laws*, trans., T. Nugent, I (1949), pp. 151, 161.
23. *The History of England*, I (1823), 16, 197, 198 (1st ed., 1762).
24. *Decline and Fall of the Roman Empire*, I (1926), 63-64.
25. *History of England*, I (1763), XI, 273.
26. Macaulay, II, 1, 3, VI, 72.
27. *An Historical Essay on the English Constitution* (1771), pp. 32, 1-10. The authorship is uncertain though sometimes attributed to Allan Ramsay. See H. Butterfield, *George III, Lord North and the People* (1949), p. 349, n. 1.
28. *Historical Essay*, pp. 9-10, 24.
29. Cited in Butterfield, *George III*, p. 348, n. 1.
30. "A Summary View of the Rights of British America," *The Debate on the American Revolution*, 1761-1783, ed., Max Beloff (1960), p. 160.
31. *History of Jamaica*, I (1724), 6.
32. See D. B. Davis, *The Problem of Slavery in Western Culture* (Harmondsworth, 1966), p. 430.
33. *Reflections on the Revolution in France* (1790-91), World Classics, no. 112 (1907), p. 33.

CHAPTER V

1. Cited in Erik von Kuehnelt-Leddihn, *Liberty or Equality* (1952), p. 12.

2. See G. W. F. Hegel, *The Philosophy of History* (New York, Dover, 1956), pp. 103-104, 341.
3. Hansard, 3rd series, 14 (1832), 1043.
4. Cited in A. D. Culler, *The Imperial Intellect* (New Haven 1955), p. 81.
5. Lord Macaulay, *Critical and Historical Essays,* II (1877), 223 (first ed., 1835).
6. Robert Knox, *The Races of Men* (1850), p. 6.
7. Luke Owen Pike, *The English and Their Origins* (1866), p. 15.
8. Cited in Louis L. Snyder, *The Idea of Racialism* (New York, 1962), p. 60.
9. *History of the Anglo-Saxons,* I (1828), 19-20.
10. Turner, I, 204, 206-07, III, 1-2, 177-78, 184.
11. Turner, III, 488-89, 498, 499.
12. Turner, I, 604. His consideration of the reign of Edward the Confessor who, prior to the eighteenth century appeared as the most favored of the Saxon kings, was limited to a single chapter.
13. Turner, III, 437-46.
14. *Past and Present,* ed., A. M. D. Hughes (1858), pp. 240, 48 (1st ed., 1843).
15. *History of Frederick II of Prussia,* I (1872), 188, 189.
16. *The Saxons in England,* I (1876), 54.
17. See Charles Petit-Dutaillis, *Studies and Notes Supplementary to Stubbs' Constitutional History,* trans., W. E. Rhodes (Manchester, 1908), Ch. II.
18. *The Anglo-Saxon,* III (1850), 8-9; II, A, 466.
19. *Irish History and Irish Character* (Oxford, 1861), pp. 5, 18.
20. *The Roman and the Teuton* (1864), pp. 17, 338, 340.
21. *History of England,* I (1865), 12; II, 395.
22. *The English in Ireland,* I (1886), 2-5.
23. *Greater Britain: a Record of Travel in English-speaking Countries during 1866-67* (1869), Preface; I, 130, II, 405.
24. *The Expansion of England* (1883), pp. 2, 50-51.
25. *Comparative Politics* (1896), p. 25.
26. *The Growth of the English Constitution* (1876), pp. 22, 23, 29, 30.
27. *Comparative Politics,* p. 1.
28. Cited in L. P. Curtis, Jr., *Anglo-Saxons and Celts* (Berkeley, 1968), p. 29.
29. *The Making of England* (1881), p. 29.
30. *The Constitutional History of England,* I (1885), 2.
31. Cited in G. P. Gooch, *History and Historians in the Nineteenth Century* (1955), p. 320.
32. *Lectures on Early English History* (1906), p. 3.

33. *The Constitutional History of England*, I (1885), 6.
34. Cited in Gooch, p. 318.

CHAPTER VI

1. *The Whig Interpretation of History* (1951), pp. 3-4, 109.
2. Cited in J. C. Holland, "The Education of Lord Acton," Diss. (Washington, Catholic University of America, 1968), p. 26.
3. Holland, p. 28.
4. Herbert Butterfield, "Acton: His Training, Methods and Intellectual System," in A. O. Savkissian, ed., *Studies in Diplomatic History and Historiography* (1961), p. 170.
5. Butterfield, "Acton's Training," p. 178.
6. *Essays Literary and Critical* (1938), p. 13.
7. "Political Thoughts on the Church," *The History of Freedom and Other Essays*, eds., J. Figgis, R. Laurence (1909), pp. 201, 204.
8. "Political Thoughts," p. 211.
9. Cited in H. A. MacDougall, *The Acton-Newman Relations* (New York, 1962), p. 30.
10. *Political Thoughts*, p. 204.
11. *Historical Essays and Studies*, eds., J. Figgis, R. Laurence (1907), pp. 341-42.
12. *History of Freedom*, pp. 298-99.
13. C[ambridge] U[niversity] L[ibrary], Add. Mss., 4987, 60.
14. Cited in MacDougall, pp. 140, 169.
15. Cited in Owen Chadwick, *The Secularization of the European Mind in the Nineteenth Century* (Cambridge, 1975), p. 112.
16. CUL, Add. Mss., 5641.
17. Cited in H. A. MacDougall, "The Later Acton: the Historian as Moralist," *Bishops and Writers* (Wheathampstead, 1977), p. 42.
18. *Historical Essays*, p. 383.
19. Reprinted in *Essays on Freedom and Power*, ed., G. Himmelfarb (1956), p. 32.
20. CUL, Add. Mss., 5015, 70; 5015, 59.
21. *The Whig Interpretation*, p. 110.
22. CUL, Add. Mss., 4908, 174.
23. Butterfield, "Acton's Training," p. 191.

CHAPTER VII

1. Stubbs, *Constitutional History*, p. 7.
2. James Cowles Prichard, *The Natural History of Man* (1843), p. 180.

3. Max Müller, *Lectures on the Science of Language* (1861), pp. 70, 199.
4. *Biographies of Words and the Home of the Aryas* (1888), pp. 120-21.
5. *Cultural Anthropology, An Introduction to the Study of Man* (1881), pp. 112, 152.
6. *The Origin of the Aryans* (1889), pp. 4, 247.
7. *Anthropological Review*, VIII, XXIX (April, 1970), 201, 211-13.
8. John Beddoe, *The Races of Great Britain* (1885), pp. 269, 271.
9. A. H. Keane, *Man: Past and Present* (1900), pp. 532, 533.
10. N. C. Macnamara, *Origin and Character of the British People* (1900), pp. 2, 174, 227, 221.
11. Charles Darwin, *The Descent of Man* (1871). Cited in Ludwig F. Schaefer, David H. Fowler, and Jacob E. Cooke, eds., *Problems in Western Civilization: The Challenge of History* (New York, 1965), p. 622.

CHAPTER VIII

1. *The Saxon and the Celt* (1897), p. 21.
2. See his *Saxon and the Celt* (1897) and *The Germans* (1916).
3. Lloyd and Jennifer Lang, *Anglo-Saxon England* (1979), p. 1.
4. F. W. Maitland, *Constitutional History of England* (Cambridge, 1908), p. 58.
5. N. K. Chadwick, "The British or Celtic Part in the Population of England," *Angles and Britains* (Cardiff, 1963), p. 111.
6. Karl Pearson, "The Problem of Anthropology," *Scientific Monthly* (II) 1920, pp. 45-57. Cited in Snyder, *Racialism*, p. 119.
7. *Heart of Darkness* (1966), p. 8.
8. Reported in *Manchester Guardian Weekly*, 121, N. 17 (Oct., 1979), 3.

INDEX